Buddhism for a Violent World

Buddhism for a Violent World

A Christian Reflection

Elizabeth J. Harris

 EPWORTH

British Library Cataloguing in Publication data

A catalogue record for this book is available
from the British Library

978 0 7162 0652 1

The author and publisher gratefully acknowledge permission to use
'Will you come and follow me?', from *Heaven Shall Not Wait*
(Wild Goose Publications, 1987). Words by John L. Bell and
Graham Maule. Copyright © 1987 WGRG, Iona Community,
Glasgow, G2 3DH, Scotland. www.wgrg.co.uk.

Permission is requested to reproduce Thich Nhat Hanh,
'Call Me by My True Names', *The Collected Poems of Thich Nhat Hanh*,
Parallax Press, Califonia. www.parallax.org.

First published in 2010
by Epworth Press
Methodist Church House
25 Marylebone Road
London NW1 5JR

Typeset by Regent Typesetting, London
Printed and bound in Great Britain by
Lightning Source UK

Contents

Dedicated with thanks to all my Sri Lankan teachers.
Most particularly those who are no longer with us
The Venerable Ayya Khema
Sr Nyanasiri
Dr Michael Rodrigo OMI
Godwin Samararatne
The Venerable Sumedha

Acknowledgements

I am deeply indebted in writing this book to all my Sri Lankan teachers and mentors, both Christians and Buddhists. The enrichment I gained through my journey into Buddhism could not have happened without them. Of the faculty members at the Postgraduate Institute of Pāli and Buddhist Studies, I am particularly grateful to the inspirational teaching of Venerable Professor Dhammavihari (then Professor Jotiya Dhirasekera) and Professor Y. Karunadasa. I also remember with gratitude the teachers who helped me to see why I needed to meditate, Venerable Ayya Khema and Godwin Samararatne. I shall never forget the Buddhist women who did so much to introduce me to Buddhist spirituality, Hema Shah, Agnes Abeyesekera, Ratna Dias, Chitra Pieris, Princie Rajakaruna, Lorna Devaraja and Ranjani de Silva. I am also indebted to the robust conversations about Buddhism that I enjoyed with a group of western Buddhist renouncers who made Sri Lanka their home, Venerable Bhikkhu Bodhi, Venerable Sumedha, Sr Nyanasiri and Venerable Miao Kwang Sudharma. I thank all of those mentioned in this paragraph for their patience with me and their acceptance of me.

Of the Christians who helped me on my journey, I am indebted particularly to the group of pioneers who, in the middle of the twentieth century, sought to re-build trust with Buddhist and Hindu communities. I thank Aloysius Pieris SJ for his wise counsel when I felt most vulnerable and Michael Rodrigo OMI for his humour, his energy and his example. I am grateful to

Yohan Devananda for helping me to envisage a meeting between Jesus and the Buddha, and his wife Malini for her support of Buddhist nuns. I have learnt at the feet of all of these and also Paul Caspaerz SJ, Audrey Rebera with her total commitment to solidarity between women, Pauline Hensman, Nelun Gunasekera, and Chitra and Kenneth Fernando. I am also grateful to Barbara Praesoody for her friendship and hospitality.

My journey into Buddhism would also not have been possible without the support of people in Britain. I am grateful to my parents. They were wary when I first went to Sri Lanka but came to support me wholeheartedly. The Methodist Church gave me pastoral and some financial support during my time in Sri Lanka and I am particularly thankful to the Revd Swaminathan Jacob, David Cruise and Graeme Jackson. I have deep thanks also for David Temple of Christians Abroad, Kenneth Cracknell at the British Council of Churches and Paul Hunt of CMS (Church Mission Society) for their moral support and their help when I needed extra funding. To the World Council of Churches I also owe a debt for making my initial years in Sri Lanka possible.

Lastly, I thank the Epworth Press for their help in bringing this publication to birth.

Introduction

In the main room of a Christian action and research centre in Sri Lanka called Tulana is a large mural relief in baked clay. It is by a Buddhist artist, Kingsley Gunatilleke, and shows Jesus in the temple at Jerusalem (Luke 2.41–52). But he is not only questioning the Jewish elders. Ranged around him are the great religious teachers of the world: Moses, Socrates, Plato, Aristotle, Buddha, Mahavira (Jain), LaoTse, Confucius and unnamed women teachers. He is looking towards them all and behind him are his parents, trying to restrain him. It is a stunning piece that changes with the different lights of the day.

The work was the fruit of two and a half years of dialogue with Dr Aloysius Pieris SJ, Director of the Centre, and it expresses beautifully one of the principles that lies behind the mission of Tulana: that the Word of life in the world is formed through exchanges between holy people from many faiths and philosophies.[1] To put it another way, its message is that the world today needs wisdom from more than one spiritual source.

This is the message that also lies behind this book. It rests on the premise that we can be enriched and challenged by encounter with faiths other than our own and uses as a case study my own 25 years of encounter with Buddhism. It is not an easy message for some Christians. Before I took up the post of Secretary for Inter Faith Relations for the Methodist Church in 1996, a post I held for 11 years, I was interviewed for the *Methodist Recorder*, a weekly Methodist newspaper. The interviewer chose to make

1

much of my study of Buddhism. She called it 'a magnificent obsession', a term I had not used myself when speaking to her. A letter sent to the paper in response said this:

> To me as a reader of her profile, Dr Harris's Christian faith comes over as a luke-warm 'also ran'. I hope for all our sakes, that I have been given the wrong impression ... Apart from any personal rewards we receive, many of us are being made aware that many of the 'riches' which people enthuse about from other faiths are to be found deep within the Christian tradition. If we hold on to that view and set about educating ourselves, the temptation to be lured by other faiths is less likely to occur – and we are in a better position to help those who are so enticed.[2]

The writer's evident conviction was that Christianity possessed a spiritual heritage that could match every other faith and that this made exploration of what other religions could give to humanity, superfluous.

I disagreed with her profoundly then and I continue to do so. We are at a point in world history when we need wisdom from many sources, if the human family is to survive and prosper. The religions of the world – not just one, but all – are one of these sources. To explore a religion not one's own, therefore, need have nothing to do with being enticed or allured, or of not knowing one's own tradition well enough. Rather, it takes the plural world we live in seriously. It recognizes the time-worn wisdom that the person who knows only one religion knows none.

My journey into Buddhism began in 1984, when I visited Sri Lanka for the first time and had what I now call an encounter with the Buddha. It developed during a period of residence in Sri Lanka during 1986–93 and continues to this day. I now teach Buddhist Studies, along with other topics in religious studies, at Liverpool Hope University. Throughout my years of encounter,

I have remained a Christian. However, I have brought into my spiritual journey insights from Buddhism that have helped me profoundly and which I believe have a message for all, Buddhist and non-Buddhist. Buddhism, in short, has become part of my life, personally and professionally.

This book aims to steer a middle path between the academic and the personal. In my academic writings on Buddhism, I have aspired to scholarly objectivity, while recognizing that true objectivity is rarely possible.[3] In my more autobiographical writings, I have struggled with what encountering 'the other' at depth has meant for me, finding that the process has been disturbing, complex and multi-faceted.[4] This book ploughs a furrow between the two.

Chapter 1 reflects on the personal side of my journey into Buddhism, giving an outline of my encounter and the context in which it took place. It aims to signpost what happened and to communicate some of the joys and anguish I experienced as I journeyed into a new way of seeing the world in a country that was moving towards full-blown internal war. The chapters that follow describe aspects of Buddhism that I have found particularly challenging or useful. Chapter 2 explores the Buddhist view of the world, concentrating on the presence of greed and hatred. Chapter 3 examines the Buddhist path and addresses particularly the western stereotype that it concerns withdrawal from rather than engagement with the world. Chapter 4 takes one aspect of the path, meditation, and argues, for instance, that the Buddhist practice of 'bare attention' or mindfulness contains something within it that is essential for human wholeness. Chapter 5 moves into how Buddhists understand one of the most intractable characteristics of our world: the existence of violence and conflict.

These chapters are less personal and give an introduction to Buddhism but they are not written purely for an academic audience and the personal is certainly not absent. My selection of topics is intimately connected with my own, engaged, spiritual journey and how Buddhism radically challenged and developed the three 'passions' or interests that I brought to my encounter with Buddhism: the use of silence in contemplative prayer and meditation; religion and social action; religions in encounter with each other. Most important also is that they draw on conversation and experience.

I do not, in these chapters, make many explicit comparisons with Christianity. This is because I would prefer Buddhism to speak for itself, albeit mediated through my experience. No doubt readers will make their own comparisons. I also, consciously, represent Buddhism at its best. The history of Christian encounter with other religions has been marred by arrogance and contempt. Even where sympathy has been expressed, there has sometimes been a sting in the tail. I refuse to follow in these footsteps. I do, however, recognize that, as in Christianity, there is difference of opinion over certain issues within the Buddhist world and struggles in relating precept (the teaching) to practice.

Chapter 6 reflects on what my encounter with Buddhism in Asia has taught me about inter faith relations in general. Here, I draw on the lives of my Christian mentors in Sri Lanka, people such as Michael Rodrigo, Aloysius Pieris, Yohan Devananda and Audrey Rebera, who have devoted their lives to creating greater understanding between Christians and Buddhists. The Epilogue then returns to the personal and draws together what this book is attempting to convey.

In all the chapters I draw on three main sources. First are the unpublished diaries I wrote during my time in Sri Lanka, which document conversations with Buddhists, an oral tradition, historical events and personal reflections. Second are the texts of Theravāda Buddhism which are of growing importance to the tradition. They are rich in narrative and even humour, as well as philosophy. Lastly, I draw on my own writings on Buddhism that have been published elsewhere, particularly by the Buddhist Publication Society in Sri Lanka. In one sense, the book draws together what I have been writing on Buddhist–Christian encounter for the last 16 years.

The Buddhist world can be divided into two: Theravāda Buddhism and Mahāyāna Buddhism. Theravāda Buddhism is found in Burma, Cambodia, Laos, Sri Lanka, Thailand and Vietnam. It has a canon of texts, in Pāli, the roots of which can be traced back to oral transmission of the Buddha's teachings, after his death. Tradition says that they were written down in Sri Lanka in the first century BCE.[5] There are three 'baskets' in the canon: the *Sutta Piṭaka* (basket of discourses); the *Vinaya Piṭaka* (the basket of monastic discipline); the *Abhidhamma Piṭaka* (the basket of 'higher' dhamma, which deals mainly with the mind). I will draw mainly on the first of these, which has five collections or *Nikāyas*: the *Dīgha Nikāya* (Long Discourses), the *Majjima Nikāya* (Middle Length Discourses); the *Saṃyutta Nikāya* (Related Sayings), the *Aṅguttara Nikāya* (Graduated Sayings) and the *Khuddaka Nikāya* (a collection of miscellaneous books).

Mahāyāna Buddhism developed in India in the early centuries of the common era and then travelled north along the Silk Road to China and Japan, and, later, over the Himalayas to Tibet. It is now found in Bhutan, China, Japan, Korea, Nepal, Tibet and also in Vietnam. It has a vast corpus of texts, originally written in Sanskrit, but now normatively accessed in their Tibetan and Chinese translations. My encounter has mainly been with Theravāda Buddhism and it is the Pāli texts that I will draw on most. However, Mahāyāna Buddhism is not absent, owing to visits to Japan and to Samye Ling, the largest Tibetan Buddhist centre in Europe, on the borders of Scotland.

To Buddhists who might read this book, I would ask pardon for any misrepresentations that you may detect. I write as a Christian who has drawn deeply from Buddhist wells in my spiritual journey. I have tried to be true to the Buddhist tradition as I have experienced it in all its variety and complexity. I am deeply grateful to my Buddhist teachers, on whose thought and teaching I have drawn, some of whom are mentioned in the acknowledgements. My thanks to them is without measure. Responsibility for any unintended misrepresentations, however, is entirely my own.

Religion at its best offers insight into why we are alive, what our task in life is and where we should place our hope. It offers tools for us to discern between what is wholesome and what is unwholesome, between what is good and what is evil. It is about life and death. The insights the different religions of the world give are not the same, although there are profound similarities between them – touching points as I prefer to call them. And some of these touching points have arisen through interaction. For no religion has grown up in isolation from other religions. Religion is a dynamic thing, changing continually as religious people interact with others and seek to re-interpret for each age the truths that they hold dear.

With this in mind, my hope is that this book may do three things. First I hope it will enable non-Buddhist readers to 'enter' Buddhism and reflect on what Buddhist insights may be able to offer a violent and disturbed world. Second, I hope it may encourage others to encounter a religion not their own, in awareness that they may have much to learn and that this learning may bring enrichment and challenge. For a book of this kind could also be written of a Christian encounter with Judaism, Islam, Hindu traditions or Sikhism, to name a few. Third, I hope that this book will offer insight and inspiration for the ongoing task of encouraging understanding, respect and joint action between people of different faiths or no identified faith.

Notes

1 See Aloysius Pieris, 1996, *Fire and Water: Basic Issues in Asian Buddhism and Christianity,* Maryknoll, NY: Orbis, pp. 136–7.

2 *Methodist Recorder*, 6 June 1996, p. 19.

3 See for instance my monograph: Elizabeth J. Harris, 2006, *Theravāda Buddhism and the British Encounter: Religious, Missionary and Colonial Experience in Nineteenth-Century Sri Lanka*, Abingdon and New York: Routledge.

4 See for instance, Elizabeth J. Harris, 2004, 'The Other Within' in Robert Crusz, Marshal Fernando and Asanga Tilakaratne (eds), *Encounters with the Word: Essays to Honour Aloysius Pieris*, Colombo: Ecumenical Institute for Study and Dialogue, pp. 331–50.

5 As a way of acknowledging the religiously plural world we inhabit, I refer to CE (Common Era) and BCE (before Common Era), rather than BC (before Christ) and AD (*Anno Domini*; the year of the Lord).

1

The Journey

Will you come and follow me
if I but call your name?
Will you go where you don't know
and never be the same?
will you let my love be shown,
will you let my name be grown
in you and you in me?[1]

In 1984 I visited Sri Lanka with a Christian group called Christians Aware. We went to the ancient pilgrimage city of Anuradhapura in north-west Sri Lanka. Between the third century BCE and the ninth century CE, it was one of the most influential Buddhist monastic centres in Asia. After the city was abandoned in the ninth century because of invasions from South India, it fell into ruins. Only in the nineteenth century were the remains re-claimed from the jungle. It can boast one of the oldest trees in the world, believed to have grown from a cutting of the original tree under which the Buddha gained enlightenment, said to have been brought from India to Sri Lanka by Venerable Sanghamitta, a Buddhist *bhikkhuṇī* or nun, in the third century BCE.

It was here that I had my first 'encounter' with the Buddha. At one point, I stole away from the group and re-entered the shrine room adjacent to this sacred tree. Devotees, dressed in white, were sitting or prostrating silently. Away from the sun's glare, the room was shadow filled. I sat on the floor with them and looked towards an image of the Buddha, which showed the Buddha sitting in meditation, against a painted scene of pale blue sky, white

clouds and mountains. As I looked, absorbing the incredible stillness of the room, the image seemed to grow larger and to glow
with light. The mountains became the cosmos. It was as though
the image beckoned to me. Against the blue of a painted sky,
the serene head became suffused with the transcendent. It was a
strange moment – a breaking in of 'the other'. Eastern religions
speak of *darsana* or *darshan* – a seeing of the holy. I had no idea
what it meant at the time. I came out of that room puzzled but
knowing that there was unfinished business between the Buddha
and me.[2]

When this happened, I had been involved in intercultural
encounter for over a decade. I was on the staff of an ecumenical
organization, Christians Abroad, counselling and advising people
who wanted to work overseas. In doing this, I drew on the time
I had spent in Jamaica, in my twenties, teaching at a government
high school. And I was already involved in inter faith encounter
in Britain as a member of a new inter faith group in Harrow,
north-west London, and what was then the World Conference
on Religion and Peace (WCRP).[3] I was beginning to realize that
the next step in my long-standing commitment to intercultural
learning was inter-religious encounter. On return from Sri Lanka,
however, my experience in Anuradhapura receded. Other concerns took over. It was awakened in 1985, when Kenneth Cracknell, then Executive Secretary of the Committee for Relationships
with People of Other Faiths at the British Council of Churches,
reported on a recent visit to Sri Lanka at a committee meeting I
was sitting through. A Christian ecumenical centre in Colombo,
he said, had just completed some study bedrooms for people
from the West who wanted to study Buddhism. Something deep
inside me moved. I can still remember the moment. I knew one
of those students would be me.

In June 1986 I returned to Sri Lanka on a World Council of
Churches' scholarship to study Buddhism at the Ecumenical
Centre for Study and Dialogue in Colombo. In my innocence, I

thought I would be there for one year on a sabbatical that would equip me to work more effectively in inter faith relations in Britain on my return. Little did I know! One thing led to another and I stayed well over seven years.

During the period between being awarded the WCC scholarship and actually travelling to Sri Lanka, there were moments of panic. I read books by George Appleton, Christmas Humphreys, Walpola Rahula and H. Saddhatissa,[4] which bewildered and excited me in equal measure. Numerous questions went through my mind. Did I really know what I was letting myself in for? Did I really want to study a religion that seemed so different from Christianity? Would it mean compromising what was most important to me?

The moments of panic were short-lived. My previous visit to Sri Lanka, a warm memory, convinced me that I would feel at home. And, at a very deep level, in spite of opposition from my own family and some Christian colleagues, I was convinced that God was calling me to this and would not let me go. I was also well aware that I was not the first Christian to have set out on such a journey! At the same time, I was aware that what I felt called to do would not be easy. Formal Buddhist–Christian dialogue did not interest me. It was a deep, experiential encounter with Buddhism that I wanted – a journey towards seeing the world through Buddhist eyes. Any romanticism I had, though, was tempered with realism. I knew this journey would take place in a country that was wracked with a bloody, brutal and long-standing ethnic conflict, and marred by a massive gap between rich and poor. I wrote this for a Christian magazine before I travelled:

Inter faith action is important for the church not because it has lost its foundations or is unsure of its message but because it is a world faith living among other faiths and sharing common concerns with them such as the wish for a more just and righteous society . . . Perhaps the most important need is that we should be open with one another, share our beliefs in a non-threatening atmosphere of honesty and be willing to learn from one another. In addition we should act together. We are in a world nearing crisis because of the forces ruling it. There is a need for all people who believe in something more than the material to work together for peace and justice . . .

Why have I chosen Buddhism? For me, the fruits of Buddhism are particularly attractive: the fruits which arise from the five precepts and the Eight-Fold Path such as compassion, selflessness and the practice of extending loving kindness to the whole of creation, including one's enemies . . . I also consider the context of Sri Lanka to be important for my study. Sri Lanka is at the cutting edge of what is happening in inter faith relationships.[5]

In addition to my interests in intercultural and inter faith encounter, I also brought two other major concerns to Sri Lanka: spirituality and contemplative prayer, and action for social justice. In the years before 1986 my Christian spiritual life had been renewed through Ignatian techniques of prayer and contemplation. I had also been accepted as an Associate Member of the Iona Community, and was attracted particularly by its justice and peace commitments. In addition, I was a keen supporter of Christian Aid, Christian CND (Campaign for Nuclear Disarmament) and the Peace Tax Campaign. It had, in fact, been Christianity's concern for social justice that had brought me back to Christianity in my early twenties, after a period of atheism. These concerns remained with me throughout my time in Sri Lanka, expressing themselves in different ways at different times.

The first year

The backbone of my first year in Sri Lanka was a Diploma in Buddhist Studies at the Postgraduate Institute of Pāli and Buddhist Studies of the University of Kelaniya. The Institute had been founded to enable foreign students to study Buddhism in Sri Lanka, through the English medium. Its first Director, Professor Jotiya Dhirasekera, was keen to stress that it was an academic institute for the study of Buddhism and not a Buddhist institute. I was part of a mixed batch of students, all mature, mostly Buddhist but with a handful of Christians and Hindus. I was the only European but not the only woman. From that fixed point, I moved outwards.

Through a friend of a friend in England, I was introduced to a group of women meditators, all Sri Lankan, and a weekly meditation session, held in a home, lead by a Buddhist monk. I met the head of my local Buddhist *vihāra* (monastery), Venerable Gnanabhiwansa, and attended the Sunday *pūjas* (acts of devotion) held during *Vassa*, the rainy season, when monks are expected to remain in one place – a period that happily coincided with my first months in Sri Lanka. This led to other invitations: to go on pilgrimage to Kataragama, a shrine in the south of the country holy to the God Kataragama, who is revered by both Sinhala Buddhists and Tamil Hindus; to attend *Pirit* sessions when monks (*bhikkhus*) chant texts believed to bring protection and blessing; to take part in *Poya* Day (Full Moon Day) observances. I also made a strong link with a Buddhist meditation centre at Nilambe in the central hills of the country. What I was doing fell broadly into four categories: formal study of the Buddhist texts and tradition; meditation using Buddhist techniques; experience of the devotional practices and day to day living of Sri Lankan Buddhists; conversations with Buddhist leaders, teachers and lay people. In other words, through an academic lens, I was encountering most of Buddhism's 'dimensions' from the doctrinal to the ritual, the institutional to the material?[6] In addition, I spoke with Christians who were in dialogue with Buddhists, secular human rights activists and members of communities where people of different religions worked together.

At the beginning, three methodological questions were important: Should I tell the Buddhists I was with that I was a Christian? How far should I observe and how far should I participate in Buddhist devotion and meditation? And, in meditation, how far should I let go of Christian methods of contemplation familiar to me in order to use Buddhist methods? My questions were not dissimilar to the questions academic researchers face when doing fieldwork in religion as a participant/observer. For me, however, the boundaries I was pushing, at this point, related to inter faith encounter rather than academic research, and to what John S. Dunne has called 'passing over' into another faith in order to 'come back', terms I only became aware of after returning to Britain in 1993.

My gut feeling was that I would learn more about Buddhism if Buddhists saw me simply as a westerner who was interested in Buddhism – a spiritual seeker – than if I stated openly that I was a Christian. I was not aware then of the extent of the mistrust towards Christians in the country but knew instinctively that the dynamics of my encounter would change if I was labelled a Christian. I decided to tell those who became close friends, but not everyone. Sri Lankan Christian friends involved in Buddhist–Christian encounter supported me in this. One academic colleague, Professor Anthony Fernando, a Christian married to a Buddhist, suggested that to identify myself as a Christian would be to reduce myself and my identity. To be truly open to Buddhism, I should let go. Dr Aloysius Pieris SJ, whom I eventually looked towards as a spiritual director, had the same advice. 'Do not label', was his advice. And he was speaking from his own experience. In his younger days, under the direction of his Buddhist teacher, he had stayed incognito in a Buddhist *vihāra* and had even been mistaken for a former *bhikkhu* because of his knowledge of Pāli.

He had also had a very special baptism into Indian religions on a visit to India.[7]

One of my first encounters with Buddhism in practice was at my local *vihāra*, Suvisudharamaya. First of all, I went to see the head monk, Ven. Wellawatte Ghanabhiwansa. I was so much the learner at that point that I had no idea when to take off my shoes or whether I should knock at any door for my appointment. As I walked in, though, an elderly monk detached himself from a group of monks in a room giving onto the *vihāra* grounds and walked towards me. He led me into a small room adjoining the *bana* (preaching) hall and bade me sit below him on what looked like a chair from a junior school. 'Lay people have to sit at a lower level to the *bhikkhu*', he explained. We spoke about my study and, wisely, he suggested that the *vihāra* could complement this, by teaching me what people do. I was warmly invited for the weekly *pūjas* – acts of devotion.

I felt very much the observer at the first *pūja*. It was a *Bodhi Pūja* that began as day ceded to the evening, followed by *Pirit*. There are three main components to a Buddhist *vihāra* in Sri Lanka: a white, often bell-shaped, *dagoba* or stupa, containing relics of some kind; a bodhi tree – the same kind of tree as the one under which the Buddha gained enlightenment; the image house, containing images of the Buddha and possibly his principle disciples. There is also a *bana* (preaching) hall, the monks' living quarters and sometimes a *dēvāle*, a shrine to the gods.[8] When I arrived, a line of women, men and children was stretched from the preaching hall to the bodhi tree. Not everyone wore white, the traditional colour worn by lay people when they visit *vihāras*. Most eyes moved towards me – the only westerner present – as I walked in. Should I join the line, I wondered to myself, and if so where? Was there a hierarchy? I assumed not and slotted myself in, placing my palms together as the others were doing. From within the hall, the head priest looked up and nodded in recognition. I wrote at the time:

15

Children were carrying aluminium pots of liquid along the line, to be sprinkled at the foot of the tree. Everyone stretched out fingers to touch whatever was brought along and then returned their hands to the 'hands together' position – reverence, not prayer, I told myself. Bowls of flowers – white, red, purple, yellow – then passed from hand to hand. The stems had been removed so that only the blooms lay, petals open, against the plastic. The line then changed direction and snaked towards the image house. Again it became a conveyor belt. Vases of anthirrhinums and greenery passed along it and then bowl after bowl of flowers, each blessed by hands, united in a common act of reverence. Again, the line changed, this time pointing towards the *dagoba* and the 28 Buddhas (Theravāda Buddhists believe that there were 28 Buddhas before Siddhartha Gotama, each serving a different era). In front of each alcove was placed a carton of artificial red flowers and a bowl of fresh blooms. Throughout, a young girl dressed in green, stood apart, chanting verses from a book.[9]

The chanting of *Pirit* that followed the *pūja* took place in the preaching hall. I knew the word *Pirit* meant 'protection' or 'safety'. I knew the ceremony would include the chanting of certain Buddhist texts, thought to ward off danger and bring blessing to the listeners. I sat with the others on a mat and observed the four monks who entered to chant, holding bamboo fans over part of their faces.

Before the chanting began, a white thread was unravelled. It circled the neck of a large, covered urn full of water, passed through the hands of the monks and then wound through the fingers of all of us. I saw it as a powerful symbol of community but wondered whether others interpreted it in this way. For the others around me, it might simply have been a tangible way of connecting with the protection inherent in the words. As for the chanting itself, I didn't find it uplifting, not that first time, only rather alien. I was rather relieved when the string was re-wound and the voices faded. Welcoming eyes, however, prevented me leaving as an isolated figure. The women especially embraced me with their eyes and touched my hands. I can remember feeling elated as I let the light of my torch guide me home.

Just a week later, I felt much more at home. I wrote this in my diary:

Last night I was again at the temple with the feeling that I was venerating the Buddha because I wanted to, not because I was copying the actions of others. Am I right to feel that I can both love Jesus and also give reverence to the Buddha as a great and compassionate teacher?[10]

That second time, I was much more the participant than the observer. The chanting seemed less alien and I was empathetic towards what happened after the chanting stopped and the white thread was re-wound. People lined up to receive some of the water in their cupped hands and have a piece of the white thread tied around their wrists. Some drank the water; most touched their faces with it. As the water poured into my own hands, I knew it represented my wish to be part of the people there. And the change from observer to participant was linked with what was happening in the other encounters with Buddhism that I was having.

During my first year in Sri Lanka, I came to appreciate the devotion of the people at quite a deep level. The atmosphere of devotion in Sri Lankan *vihāras* is palpable, tangible. It glows. For the Buddha is seen by Asian Buddhists as much more than a human teacher. He is the embodiment of wisdom and compassion, the embodiment of the highest truth and of supreme holiness. There has been a strand in western writing on Buddhism that has stressed that Buddhism is only a philosophy of life. Anyone who has sympathetically witnessed Buddhism in practice in Asia must disagree. As Venerable Ananda Metteyya (Allan Bennett), the second British person to become a Buddhist monk, declared to a western audience at the beginning of the twentieth century, after living in Burma:

> For you must understand that this is no mere cut-and-dried philosophy – as it may seem to one who reads of it out here in books – but a living, breathing Truth; a mighty power able to sweep whomsoever casts himself wholeheartedly into its great streams, far and beyond the life we know and live.[11]

There are different forms of devotion in Sri Lankan Buddhism. The kind of *pūja* that I witnessed is just one. On Full Moon Days (Poya Days), some lay people will spend the whole day at their local *vihāra* and follow eight guidelines for conduct, including not eating after noon, to bring their lifestyle closer to the monastic. The *vihāra* provides a set programme of sermons, given by different *bhikkhus*, guided meditations and periods for reading or one's own practice. The day will begin just as dawn lightens the sky with the raising of a Buddhist flag. A *bhikkhu/s* will then lead a chanted salutation to the Buddha, followed by the chanting of the eight precepts of conduct.

In addition to the corporate devotion seen during *Vassa* and on *Poya* Days, people will come to the *vihāras* for personal, individual devotion. They will first go to the *dagoba*, since this represents the Buddha, and circumambulate it clockwise, chanting from the texts. Next they will honour the Bodhi tree. In some temples, where there is room, people might sit and meditate close to it, as the Buddha is said to have done after his enlightenment. Lastly, they will enter the shrine room, place flowers on a ledge in front of the images and prostrate. Light and incense may also be offered outside. Most *vihāras* have iron stacks where lighted oil lamps can be placed. This type of devotion means that there are always people in the *vihāras*. Individual devotion, however, also takes place in the home, since many Buddhists have their own shrines to the Buddha.

Devotional practices in most Asian Buddhist countries are seen as distinct from what outsiders often link with Buddhism – meditation. And it was meditation that presented me with some of the deepest challenges. Although I had spent time at Christian retreat centres and had practised some of the Ignatian Exercises, the idea of sitting in silence in a Buddhist context intimidated me. It took courage to walk into my first session of Buddhist meditation. It was in the house of a middle class lay Buddhist, a Mrs de Silva, lasted over an hour and was led by a *bhikkhu*. There were just seven of us, sitting on cushions in a circle. We were told to concentrate on the air touching the inside of our nostrils and to notice the arising and passing of thoughts and feelings. At one point the *bhikkhu* said this, 'Resist any wish to move the body. It will hinder your concentration and you will have to begin again. Moving means you are giving in to feelings of displeasure. Feelings arise and pass. You must transcend them. If the feeling does not go, enter the feeling, make it an object of meditation, saying, "Sensation, sensation" rather than "Pain". Return to your breathing when the feeling passes.'

I came away from that first session elated, because I had remained still for an hour. The guidance that the leader gave was clear and I felt no temptation to do something more Christian. After all, there is no Christian breath or Buddhist breath. There is only breath. And I had not been asked to make any Buddhist statement of faith. The crisis came when I was at the Buddhist Meditation Centre at Nilambe in the central hills. The location was magnificent – high, cool, with nothing but hills all around, for ever changing with the movement of light and cloud. The journey there was a pilgrimage in itself. It took over six hours from Colombo. I had neither anticipated its remoteness nor its altitude. On my first visit, the path leading from the road to the Centre seemed interminable. I had been told 15 or 20 minutes but it took 45 to negotiate the wide loops and bends with ever more beautiful glimpses of distant peaks.

The schedule each day began at 5.00 a.m. and was strictly regulated but there was freedom within the meditation sessions for people to experiment with different meditation methods. In the beauty of the surroundings, my first wish was to praise God, to see God in the hills. I wrote this in my diary:

> The sessions in the meditation hall are a challenge. We sit on either side like lines of solitary Buddhas. There is no communication between us. In Buddhist thought, we cannot give insight to one another. At times, I've been filled with impatience: impatience at the immovable stillness of the others, impatience at the idea of some of them doing this for months on end or the idea of me doing it for another hour. I've also felt tension between what my soul wants to do as a Christian and what the aim seems to be in Buddhism. I've wanted to reach out to the love at the heart of creation. I've wanted to imagine God's grace, Spirit and strength flowing through me. In Buddhist insight (*vipassanā*) meditation, however, the aim is to realize the truth of impermanence (*anicca*) and no-soul (*anattā*). Do I want to reach such a realization? Part of me says no. Yet, at the same time, the value of bare attention, the watching of thoughts and sensations, seems essential to self-knowledge and growth. And are there not certain links between *anicca* and *anattā* and some Christian insights? That we are made of dust; that we are no-thing in ourselves; that the world (although created good) is subject to change, destruction ...' [12]

Godwin Samararatne, the lay Director and meditation teacher at Nilambe, had encouraged us to use a form of meditation that he called, 'bare attention'. It was a meditation of awareness rather than concentration. We were to allow thoughts and feelings to arise freely in our minds and our bodies without controlling or willing them. We were to observe them as if they belonged to someone else and allow them to arise and pass. I will say more about this in a later chapter. As in the sessions in Colombo, no Buddhist statement of faith was involved. It was a practice that both Buddhists and non-Buddhists could do, albeit in a room containing an image of the Buddha.

As my time at Nilambe lengthened, the urge to use Christian categories lessened but it was not until a couple of months afterwards that I wrote categorically, 'in order to enter Buddhism, I must "let go" so that my mind begins to use the categories of Buddhism without continually leaping back to Christian ways of thought'.[13] If I was to see the world through Buddhist eyes, I could not cling conceptually to Christianity. Most particularly, since Buddhism is essentially a non-theistic religion, my default position in meditation, an orientation towards God, had to shift or go into hibernation.

A significant point in this process of letting go came for me in December 1986 in a conversation about meditation with Aloysius Pieris. We were talking about how we should deal with the thoughts and feelings that arise in meditation. Fr Aloy, as his friends call him, was comparing Buddhist methods with those of St Ignatius and St John of the Cross. He encouraged me to take a non-judgemental approach. Most of all, he suggested, I should stop using Christian categories. 'The desire to put a Christian interpretation on experiences is again a tendency to place the past on the present', he stressed. Our conversation covered many other things. When I asked him at the end whether he had any other guidance to give me, he said, 'No, you're doing all right.' He added, 'To walk through the desert without fear is to be truly a Christian.'[14]

Those words touched me deeply. For the process of letting go had, by that time, led me into some desert experiences. However, it had also brought me much joy as I gave myself to a new vocabulary and a new way of seeing. I was beginning to realize that if I truly answered, 'Yes' to the challenge of letting go, then the beauty of Buddhism would truly begin to flower.[15]

The process of immersing myself in Buddhism was given a boost when I travelled to Bodh Gaya in India in February 1987 for the first international conference on Buddhist nuns. Bodh Gaya, near Gaya in north-east India, is where Buddhists believe the Buddha gained enlightenment. Most Buddhist countries have a monastery and pilgrim centre there. A Buddhist friend in Sri Lanka, Dr Hema Gunatileke, had encouraged me to go. The conference was organized by Professor Chatsumarn Kabilsingh (Thai), Venerable Karma Kekshe Tsomo (American *bhikkhunī* in the Tibetan tradition) and Sr Ayya Khema (German Buddhist nun ordained into the Sri Lankan tradition). The conference coincided with a visit of His Holiness, the Dalai Lama to Bodh Gaya so there was a very large group of Tibetan monks and nuns there and many of the nuns attended. In addition, Buddhist nuns and lay women came from America, many European countries, Nepal, Taiwan, Vietnam, Burma and, of course, Sri Lanka.

Since I had only had exposure to the Buddhism of Sri Lanka, it was disorienting at first to meet Buddhists from other traditions. But I was not the only one to be disorientated. A good number of Buddhist women there had never met Buddhists from other schools of Buddhism. So a large amount of time was spent simply on country reports about the position of women, particularly ordained women. For, at that time, there was a division between those countries where women could gain higher ordination (*upasampadā*) such as Taiwan and Vietnam, and those where higher ordination had died out or had never existed such as Burma, Sri Lanka, Tibet and Thailand. In Tibet, women could only receive a novice ordination and, in Sri Lanka, they could receive a ten precept ordination and become *dasa sil māthās* (ten precept mothers). This was in contrast to the over 300 rules of the full *bhikkhunī* discipline.

As far as my own journey was concerned, the intensity and the enthusiasm of the nuns and lay people deeply affected me. Their principal aim was for Buddhist nuns from across the world to be able to greet one another in unity. A close second, though, was the eventual restoration of the *bhikkhuṇī* order in countries where it no longer existed. I wrote at the time, 'I find myself encouraging and affirming the nuns. How difficult Christians at home would find this! Yet how can I not support these people, who are so full of love and all the fruits of the spirit.' Yet, as at Christian conferences, there were divisions and misunderstandings, and participants who seemed to want power. I was particularly aware of prejudice among some Mahāyāna nuns towards those from Theravāda countries, and also of the vast difference in economic status between nuns and lay Buddhist women from the West, and those from countries such as Tibet. One positive outcome of the Conference was the founding of Sakyadhita (lit: Daughters of the Buddha) an international Buddhist women's organization, of which I became a founder member.

After the Conference, many of the participants went on pilgrimage to Buddhist sites in India. There was an expensive and a cheap alternative. I chose the cheap one, which meant sleeping in Buddhist centres and temples rather than hotels, together with the Tibetan nuns and others who could not afford to spend too much. At Ballrampur, we, in the 'second bus', had no confirmed accommodation, while those in the 'first bus' were housed in a luxurious colonial-type mansion. A Buddhist centre was found for us, and we were taken into an empty, dusty hall with a shrine room at the end. While we had a meal of chapatti, dahl and vegetable curry at a local eating place, it was transformed. We came back to individual mosquito nets and clean linen. My patch was in the shrine room at the feet of the Buddha, a remarkably evocative space. It was strange but somehow wonderful, in the morning, to wake up and look into the contours of the white Buddha image and to hear, as on all the other mornings, the Tibetan nuns chanting their morning devotions.

Most who went on the pilgrimage had to struggle with illness and tiredness, me included. The whole visit to India was one of the most intense and tiring experiences of my life. Yet, it brought me close to Buddhist spirituality and the complexity within world Buddhism in a way that no other experience could. At the end, I travelled, alone, to two more Buddhist sites in India: Sanchi and the caves at Ajanta, filled with Buddhist and Jain images. At this point, I could actually imagine myself a Buddhist nun – or rather, could imagine myself 'renouncing' in a radical way, so deeply had I internalized monastic spirituality.

Sanchi was an absolute gem. Its Buddhist monuments go back to the third century BCE with a stupa that was thought to be commissioned by Emperor Asoka. Most of the monuments, though, are later. Its Buddhist life stretched to the twelfth century CE. At the time of my visit, Sanchi was a sleepy, undeveloped village. I attracted little unwanted attention, dressed in *salwar kameez* and *saree*, and simply absorbed. I stayed at the 'railway retiring rooms', advertised in the Lonely Planet Guide as the best in India – armchairs, mosquito nets, shower room, washroom and toilet room. I wrote in my diary:

My eyes have feasted on first-century BC stonework. I could spend hours, just looking at the carvings on the four gateways to the main stupa: royal processions, Jataka stories, scenes from the Buddha's life – all in a condensed intensity of shape and form. A stupa or a bodhi tree represents the Buddha. In medieval times and before, the plateau was covered in monasteries. Now the flies buzz around foundation walls, the bases of pillars, fallen columns ... but there is a spirituality present – perhaps from all the mind training, all the renunciation and compassion that has been expressed here. But I could be idealising! The Asokan pillar here warns the monastic Sangha of schism, and there is evidence of destruction by fire.[16]

Back in Sri Lanka, feeling 'older', for the whole visit had been both joy and struggle, I had exams to prepare for and was not free to follow every Buddhist encounter that offered itself. I devoted myself to reading the Pāli texts, my lecture notes and secondary sources. Sri Lanka was also moving into a new phase of the ethnic conflict. In April 1987, a bomb placed by Tamil terrorists, most probably the Liberation Tigers of Tamil Eelam (LTTE), exploded in a taxi in Pettah, one of the most crowded parts of downtown Colombo, killing 100 people and injuring many more. As a result, Vesak, the most important full moon day of the year, in May, when Buddhists celebrate the birth, death and enlightenment of the Buddha, was a muted event. For instance, there were far fewer *pandols*, which are massive temporary wooden structures, erected at road intersections, that narrate Buddhist stories through pictures and lights. Then on 2 June, 31 Buddhist monks were hacked to death as they were travelling from the East of the country, Ampara, to a peace march in Kataragama. A log was placed across the road. The driver was forced to take the bus into the jungle, where the monks where shot and hacked to death in their seats: cold horror and a foretaste of things to come.

In the weeks following, there was also a growing fear of the militancy of a southern Sinhala group, the Janatha Vimukthi Peramuna (The Peoples' Liberation Front or JVP),[17] which claimed to be Marxist, promised radical change and sought government overthrow. It was attracting Sinhala-educated rural youth, disillusioned with a system that gave priority to English.

The centre of my *Vesak* was a small group of seven women who met at home with a schedule of meditation, discussion and reading that was as strict as if they were in a *vihāra*. They had asked me to talk to them about some of the Buddha's discourses that I found meaningful. I wrote at the time, 'The strangeness of it hits me! I, a Christian, gave them a talk about some of the fundamentals of Buddhism as I saw them and felt quite at home.' I chose four discourses (*suttas*) that conveyed something of what I had learnt in the last year. These included the *Cakkavatti Sīhanāda Sutta* and the *Kakacūpama Sutta*, which I will mention in later chapters. It is enough to say now that they touched both on Buddhism's socially engaged message and on meditation, two of the interests I had brought to Sri Lanka but which also found me as I read the Buddhist texts.

I left Sri Lanka after my first year in June 1987, knowing that I would return. The Methodist Church in Britain had asked me to stay on for a second year to fill a Methodist visa before another mission partner arrived. At that time, each church had a limited number of visas. If they were not filled, they vanished. I accepted on the condition that I could continue my study of Buddhism, progressing from my successfully completed Postgraduate Certificate to the MA. Waiting at the airport at 4.00 a.m, I wrote:

My mind is full. Part of me wants to rush back to Colombo. I have been heaped with kindness and presents of all kinds. I have become involved with the very texture of life here, with its contradictions, its tensions, its hopes and its anguish. I have seen the pride and the devotion of the Sinhalese towards their culture, language and religion and their fear that Buddhism might be threatened by outside forces. I have been made aware that this very pride and fear has a negative side that can be twisted into racism. I have opened myself to Sri Lankan villagers, their struggles and their devotion. I have eagerly talked with concerned activists who are trying to find relevance in religion for their struggle for justice. I have questioned together with those Buddhists who are questioning.[18]

The second year

My return to the country for the second year was marked by curfew and smoke. It was the day after 18 had been killed and over 100 injured at a protest against an imminent Peace Accord with India, which would bring a system of Provincial Councils to the country and, so it was thought, a peace overseen by an Indian Peacekeeping Force (IPKF). It was seen as a sign of hope by some but both the LTTE and the JVP were to reject it.

During my second year, I combined cataloguing the archival material at the Sri Lankan Methodist Church headquarters with study. I continued to meditate at Nilambe, to read the Pāli texts and to visit my local *vihāra*. Not long into my second year, though, two internal wars were threatening the stability of the country. In the north, the Indian Peacekeeping Force was fighting the LTTE, after it had rejected the Peace Accord. In the south, government forces were trying to control the JVP, which, by this time, had launched a full-scale uprising, targeting as traitors to the motherland supporters of the Peace Accord.

There is not scope within this chapter to detail the JVP uprising. What was important for my journey into Buddhism was that I was brought face to face experientially with the First Noble Truth in Buddhism, the Noble Truth of *dukkha* through the violence, intimidation and sheer brutality of the JVP and the equally brutal response of the government. The JVP and its military wing, the DJV (Deshapremi Janatha Vyaapaaraya – Patriotic People's Movement) tried to gain power through targeted assassinations and the calling of strikes, enforced by death threats, to bring the country to its knees economically. One of its targets was the 'old left', leaders and members of the Marxist parties formed in the middle of the twentieth century, most of whom supported the Peace Accord or at least a political solution to the ethnic conflict.

Particularly poignant for me, in my second year, was the killing, in October 1987, of Fr Michael Rodrigo, a Roman Catholic priest who had chosen to work in a remote Buddhist village in the south of the country. He had become one of my mentors and I say much more about him in Chapter 6. His killers were never identified.

Many others I knew were under threat in this period. The crucial question for me was how I should deal spiritually and emotionally with this threat to people I had come to hold dear. How far should I become vulnerable to the suffering of others? Reflecting on this, I gradually noticed a change in my attitude to Buddhism and my journey. The attraction of renunciation moved into the background to be replaced by a wish to be socially engaged and to become vulnerable to suffering. My conversations with Buddhist friends were less about meditation and more about the Law of *Kamma*, a word that literally means action in Buddhism. According to the Law, good actions produce good fruits and bad actions, bad fruits. After the Pettah bomb, a number of my Buddhist friends asked themselves, 'Were those who died suffering the fruits of previous misdeeds?' One particular friend felt compelled to believe that the Law of *Kamma* was at work in some way, although her compassion rebelled at the idea.

It was against this background that I chose for the extended piece of writing within my MA the topic of what the early Buddhist texts, the Pāli Canon, said about violence and disruption in society. By this time, I had come to love reading the Pāli texts of Theravāda Buddhism, albeit, at this point, in translation. I was particularly struck by the persona of the Buddha that arose through them. Few academics would say that the texts communicate the exact words of the Buddha. After the Buddha's death, his teachings were transmitted orally for several centuries. Changes were made to aid this process and inevitably additions crept in. Tradition says the texts were only written down in Sri Lanka, in the first century BCE. Yet, there was enough in the texts for me to glimpse the Buddha. Most of the discourses recorded in the texts show the Buddha in dialogue with others and I liked what I read. The Buddha came across to me as a realistic, down-to-earth teacher – a teacher I could revere.

The third year

Towards the end of my second year, Fr Aloysius Pieris asked me to be his Research Assistant at Tulana. It did not take me long to agree, and the Methodist Church helped to fund it. So, after another short visit to England, I returned once more to Sri Lanka in September 1988. I moved to a cottage in Kelaniya and cycled every day to Tulana. In the year that followed, my journey into Buddhism did not lead me to many new places geographically, partly because of internal war in the country, which made travel dangerous, and partly because I had less need. Buddhism had simply become part of me. So I devoted myself to cataloguing the superb antiquarian library at Tulana and researching topics such as Buddhism and slavery in Sri Lanka. Fr Aloy also encouraged me to begin working on what would become my doctorate – the encounter between the British and Buddhism in nineteenth-century Sri Lanka, particularly the missionary encounter, the consequences of which were still being experienced in Buddhist mistrust of Christianity.[19]

In the third year, fear for people threatened by the JVP was still very much part of my life. At this time a new piece of sculpture was created at Tulana by Kingsley Gunatilleke, a Buddhist artist. It was a pieta and it was direct comment on the violence in the country. Mary was moulded so that her body was similar to the shape of the island of Sri Lanka. Jesus, on her lap, was naturalistic, not ideal. Behind the figures were a military tank and a lamp post, which together made a cross. The tank represented the military and the lamp post, one mode of killing used by youth militants in the country. But as Fr Aloy pointed out to me, the lamp post was also shaped like a cobra and cobras could be tamed, as youth militants could be if their idealism was used in positive ways by the country. Fr Aloy commented in an article written later:

This sculpture has frozen in cement and stones the events of 1989 when thousands of youth lost their precious lives in a brutal conflict with the state forces. The sculptor saw in Jesus a Word of challenge and hope that speaks through these events. Mother Lanka and her youth are made to announce the paschal mystery which we call the Christ-event.[20]

At that time, I could not pass the pieta without my stomach lurching in recognition of what was happening in the country and in fear for those I knew, who were threatened.

When meditating at Nilambe in February 1989, I also had to face my fear for others, knowing that in nearby Kandy people were being killed. That period of meditation was a turning point. There is no space here to describe all I experienced. Suffice it to say that I confronted my fear head on, as one should in meditation and, eventually, touched that which is beyond fear. I believe I also took a step towards the Buddhist practice that nuns in the Tibetan tradition had explained to me, when one takes into oneself the darkness and fear of the world and radiates light in return. I wrote at the time:

To overcome fear with light is not to enter an unreal world of spiritual purity. It is to meet people where they are; to meet oneself; to accept complexity and earthiness. It is to take into oneself what it is to be human, but to be aware that darkness can be transformed.[21]

The next month, on 18 March 1989, I participated in a Martyrs' Day at Devasarana, an inter faith engaged community near Kurunegala. Devasarana had begun as a Christian ashram, under the leadership of a young Anglican priest, the Revd Yohan Devananda, in the 1950s. In the years that followed, it began to engage with the economic and political problems of the surrounding villages and became interreligious and a pioneer in social action. It became a target of the JVP because of its link with people in the established Left parties. By 1989, it had seen many of its working partners killed. In a most moving ceremony, the day commemorated 138 left-wing activists killed by the DJV. Photographs of their mutilated bodies greeted us as we entered the main room. Inside the room, though, were pictures of the murdered activists in health. The day was one of defiance and solidarity, with participants from all communities and faiths.

Another exception to my lack of travel came in July 1989, when I travelled to the pilgrimage centre of Kataragama for a *perahera* (a festival), with American researcher, Tessa Bartholomeusz. We were to witness the violence of the period first hand. As dancers and elephants moved along a pathway to take the god Kataragama to his bed with his consort, Vallee, watched by hundreds of ordinary people, who had come in lorries, trucks and vans, we heard two blasts ahead of the place where we were standing. Numbed silence followed and then confusion. A man ran, frenzied, up the pathway carrying the limp, blood-spattered body of a woman over his shoulder. Elephants were guided away with nervous hands. Dancers hastily retreated. Tessa and I, trying to remain calm, joined the crowd that was walking in numbed, anxious silence away, as ambulances and military vehicles, guns erect, headlights flashing, swept in. At one point we thought we would never get out of the holy area. There was only one exit where we were, a small bridge. People and military vehicles were both trying to use it. Numbed silence became panic. But eventually we crossed to the Rest House where we were staying. The death toll, we heard later, was 13 with 90 seriously injured. That night planes droned overhead. But, the next morning, in the holy precinct, it was as though nothing had happened. People were worshipping as usual.

The JVP uprising lasted until November 1989 when its leader, Rohan Wijeweera, was killed by government forces. The last months of the uprising were bloody with government-backed paramilitary groups and the army itself killing a generation of Sinhala youth suspected of involvement.

In 1990, I once again returned to Britain, this time to raise money to complete the doctorate Fr Aloy had encouraged me to do. I was back by December of that year to remain a further three years. I must glide over these years in this initial chapter. Much that I learnt and became involved in will appear in the chapters that are to follow – as will the ongoing post-1993 journey, when I returned to Britain and eventually encountered other forms of Buddhism in Burma, Cambodia, Japan, Thailand and, of course, Britain.

When I left Sri Lanka in 1993, Sri Lanka and the Buddhism of Sri Lanka had become part of me. Throughout my time in the country, I maintained contact with the churches and preached in the Colombo South Methodist Circuit. But I was also at home in Buddhist centres and *vihāras*. I had truly been led, in the words of John Bell's hymn, to places that I could not have imagined. And I was not the same person. Yet, as I hope the following chapters will show, the journey was one of enrichment not loss.

Notes

1 'Will you come and follow me?', hymn by John Bell of the Iona Community.

2 See also, Elizabeth J. Harris, 2000, 'My Unfinished Business with the Buddha' in Rita M. Gross and Terry C. Muck (eds), *Christians Talk about Jesus; Christians Talk about the Buddha*, London: Continuum, p. 89.

3 The WCRP was founded in 1970 and is now called the World Conference of Religions for Peace, or simply Religions for Peace.

4 I have also referred to this in: Elizabeth J. Harris, 2002, 'The Beginning of Something Being Broken: The Cost of Crossing Spiritual Boundaries' in *Spirituality across Borders*, Oxford: The Way Supplement 2002/14: 7. The books I read included: George Appleton, 1961,

On the Eightfold Path: Christian Presence among Buddhism, London: SCM Press; Christmas Humphreys, 1985 (1951), *Buddhism: An Introduction and Guide*, London: Penguin; Walpola Rahula, 1985 (1959), *What the Buddha Taught*, London: Gordon Fraser; H. Saddhatissa, 1976, *The Life of the Buddha*, London: Unwin.

5 Newsletter of the Methodist Layman's Missionary Association, 1986.

6 Ninian Smart's dimensions are: practical/ritual; experiential/emotional; narrative/mythic; doctrinal/philosophical; ethical/legal; social/institutional; material. See for example, Ninian Smart, 1989, *The World's Religions*, Cambridge and New York: Cambridge University Press.

7 See, for example, the first reflections in Aloysius Pieris, 2005, *Prophetic Humour in Buddhism and Christianity: Doing Inter-Religious Studies in Reverential Mode*, Colombo: Ecumenical Institute for Study and Dialogue (*Dialogue* 2004, vol. XXXI).

8 In Theravāda Buddhism gods are beings who reside in the heavens. They can be petitioned for mundane blessings but are below the Buddha and have nothing to do with ultimate liberation.

9 Unpublished diary, 27 July 1986.

10 Unpublished diary, 3 August 1986, this section quoted in Harris, 2002, 'The Beginning of Something Being Broken', p. 10.

11 See Elizabeth J. Harris, 1998, *Ananda Metteyya: The First British Emissary of Buddhism*, Kandy, Buddhist Publication Society, p. 51.

12 Unpublished diary, 8 September 1986, partially quoted in Harris, 2002, 'The Beginning of Something Being Broken', p. 11.

13 Unpublished diary, 14 November 1986, this part quoted in Harris, 2002, 'The Beginning of Something Being Broken', p. 11.

14 See also Harris, 2002, 'The Beginning of Something Being Broken', p. 13 and Harris, 2004, 'The Other Within' in Robert Crusz, Marshal Fernando, Asanga Tilakaratne (eds), *Encounters with the Word: Essays to Honour Aloysius Pieris*, Colombo: Ecumenical Institute for Study and Dialogue, pp. 331–50, here p. 331.

15 Harris, 2002, 'The Beginning of Something Being Broken', p. 14.

16 Unpublished diary, February 1987.

17 The JVP was founded in 1965 and mounted an armed youth

insurrection in 1971. This was crushed violently but the JVP entered the political process, only to go underground again in 1983, when it was blamed for violence against Tamils.

18 Unpublished diary, 16 June 1987.

19 The eventual title of my doctorate was: *Crisis, Competition and Conversion: The British Encounter with Buddhism in Nineteenth Century Sri Lanka*, submitted to the University of Kelaniya in 1993.

20 Aloysius Pieris, 1996, 'Inculturation in Asia: A Theological Reflection on an Experience' in Aloysius Pieris, *Fire and Water: Basic Issues in Asian Buddhism and Christianity*, Maryknoll, NY: Orbis, p. 136.

21 Unpublished diary, February 1989.

2

The Human Condition

9 June 1989 was a day during the height of the JVP insurrection. In Kandy, in the central hills, schools were closed because of
student demonstrations. Few buses were running. Women were
being told not to drape their *sarees* in the Indian way as a protest against the Peace Accord, which the JVP attributed to Indian
imperialism. The whole atmosphere was tense with fear. There
were killings and disappearances. Parents feared their young
people would be suspected of JVP involvement and taken by
government forces. People who had openly supported the Indo-
Lankan Peace Accord feared a JVP bullet or knife. It was in this
situation that I spoke to Sr Nyanasiri, an American Buddhist nun
(a ten precept nun, dressed in orange robes) living alone with her
dogs near Kandy, about human evil and fear.

'I don't think people are sinful. They are simply deluded,' she
insisted. 'People basically want to do right but they are trapped
in ignorance.' She saw the young people who were drawn to the
JVP because it promised change and greater justice as victims of
their own ignorance. Even the JVP leaders masterminding the
operation, she believed, were deluded in their confidence that a
better world would arise if the 'socialist' JVP governed the country. 'Sin' in the Christian sense did not come into the picture. It
was not alienation from God that was the problem. God did not
enter into it. It was ignorance of the true nature of existence. This
ignorance was not something to be condemned as abhorrent. It
was something to grieve over, to exercise compassion over – and,

of course, if one could, to challenge and change through education and example.

The core of the Buddha's message in the fifth century BCE was,
'The way you see the world is wrong. Change.' As one text from
the Pāli Canon puts it:

Everything the world holds good, sages see otherwise
What others call *sukha* (happiness), that the saints call *dukkha*
(suffering).[1]

A verse from the Dhammapada, a popular book within the
Khuddaka Nikāya of the Pāli Canon, puts it this way:

This world has become blind; few see here.
A few go to heaven like a bird released from a net.[2]

What most people praise is empty, these verses imply, and what
most people do is the result of delusion. When Buddhists go to
their local *vihāra* and lay flowers before images of the Buddha,
they are revering a person who not only embodied compassion
but also insisted that we should change the way we see the world
and our own existence, if we are to be liberated from spiritual
blindness. And this change goes back to what the historical Buddha, Siddhattha Gotama, 'saw' when he became enlightened in
the fifth century BCE.[3]

Dukkha: the heaven and hell of existence

The central, overriding issue for the historical Buddha was the
presence in human existence of what the Pāli language calls
dukkha. It is a word that is difficult to translate. Old age, illness,
the death of loved ones, crushed hopes, loss of wealth or possessions, and death are ways in which *dukkha* is experienced. It
encompasses suffering, pain, unsatisfactoriness and existential

anxiety. To become aware of *dukkha* is to realize that there is something deeply skewed and imperfect about human existence. It was an awareness of *dukkha*, according to the traditional narrative of the Buddha's life, which impelled the Buddha-to-be, at the age of 29, to leave his luxurious home on a spiritual search. He was brought up in an aristocratic home in one of the republics of North East India. Tradition says that he was shielded from all suffering and pain in his youth, his father fearing that he might become a spiritual rather than a worldly leader, following a prediction at his birth. However, he eventually broke through the cordon around him and ventured outside his home without the way having been prepared for him. As a result, he saw three sights that shook him to the core – a sick person, an elderly person and a corpse, symbols of our mortality and impermanence. Then he saw a holy person, one of many at that time who had renounced home and family to become a 'Wanderer', a seeker after spiritual truth.

It was this encounter, with both the suffering of life (*dukkha*) and a figure representing a spiritual way forward, so the story goes, that impelled him to leave his wife, Yasodhara, and his young son, Rahula, to become a mendicant spiritual searcher, in what Buddhists see as an act of supreme compassion for humankind. Most Buddhists would also say that it awakened within him the path he had chosen many lives past – the path towards Buddhahood. The First Noble Truth of Buddhism – or the first reality of life for the noble ones[4] – is the Noble Truth of *Dukkha*. It forms a backdrop to the Buddha's teaching.

The word *dukkha* may appear alien to the western mind. But is it? Eduard Munch's work, *The Scream*, comes close to capturing it. At the centre of the piece is a woman screaming, her mouth contorted, her eyes staring in fear, her muscles contracted, her hands held against her cheeks. The contortion of her face ripples out into the air around her so that her immediate environment echoes the scream. The piece vibrates with anguish. Tom Butler,

Anglican Bishop of Southwark, on 17 April 2007, after an incident of multiple shooting at Virginia Technical College in America the day before, referred to it on a 'Thought for the Day' on BBC Radio 4. The year of 2007, he suggested, already seemed to be the year of the scream, not only because of the Virginia Tec killing but because of the killing of young people through gun crime on London's streets, the daily deaths in Iraq and the suffering of Darfur. Buddhists would say that every year is a year of the scream. Every year people are torn apart from those they love. Every year young life is lost. Every year war takes its terrifying toll. And every year, each human being moves inexorably towards death.

Käthe Kollwitz (1867–1945) is another European artist who vividly portrayed what Buddhists would call *dukkha*. Käthe lost her son, Peter, in the First World War in 1914 and became a life-long opponent of war. One of her drawings shows a mother with her children peeping warily from underneath the folds of her long dress. The mother's strong, muscular arms are stretched out in protection over her children. But her eyes survey the distance fearfully for any threat, knowing that children cannot be protected from war, death or suffering. Kollwitz was able to portray joy – the joy of motherhood, for instance – but her art is overwhelmingly about hardship, oppression, war, ageing and death.

It is with images such as Munch's scream and Kollwitz's pictures of war and death that Buddhist philosophers begin when reflecting on the human condition. Buddhism does not deny that there is beauty and happiness in the world but it points to the impermanence of the things that most people turn to for happiness or hope – status, a good job, possessions, security, beauty or handsomeness, or even political change. Buddhism in fact speaks of three characteristics of existence: impermanence (*anicca*), *dukkha* and non-self (*anattā*). Everything in the world (except the goal of the spiritual life, *nibbāna*) is impermanent, even the self. There is nothing in the human body or mind that is not subject to change, nothing that can be extracted from the human person as an immortal, unchanging essence. Everything arises and passes away. The problem, according to Buddhism, is that most people act as though this were not so, as though the next project will give them all that they need for happiness, as though they will never age, never lose their possessions or their health, never suffer misfortune. Perhaps most important of all, many people act as though death will not come, that time will not pass as quickly for them as for others. In Pāli, there is a word for one of the 'many-folk', the ordinary people – *puthujjana*. It is a word that can either mean 'several/ many' or 'separate/ individual'. A *puthujjana* is invariably seen as deluded. In contrast, one who seeks to follow the way of the Buddha would train herself not to see any phenomena subject to change as permanent, as happiness, as the self. One text puts it this way:

> It is impossible, monks, it cannot come to pass, that a person who is possessed of (right) view should regard any one phenomenon as permanent. But monks, it is quite possible for the undeducated manyfolk (*puthujjana*) to do so.[5]

This is the kind of ignorance that Sr Nyanasiri believed the idealistic JVP supporters were trapped in. Another way of looking at *dukkha* is to see it as arising from the continual tension between opposites: love and hatred; attraction and repulsion; beauty and ugliness; sadness and joy. I had long been aware of this tension when I met Buddhism. In the 1970s, when teaching in Jamaica, the contrast between the almost unbelievable beauty of the island and its problems, most particularly the gap between rich and poor, gun crime and political violence, leapt out at me. There was a snake in paradise, I decided, an ever-present struggle, an ever-present sadness. Buddhists would call it *dukkha*.

In my first year in Sri Lanka, this tension came home to me again, forcibly, as the previous chapter explains. But let me give another example. In April 1987, a friend from France came to Sri Lanka for a holiday. We travelled by bus to the ancient ruined Buddhist capital, Polonnaruwa, and stayed at the 'Rest House', overlooking the ancient man-made tank or lake. Sri Lanka's early civilization excelled in its management of water through building 'tanks' or lake-like reservoirs. It was peaceful and sublimely beautiful. And Polonnaruwa itself made a great impact on us, especially the Gal Vihāra (Stone Monastery) where three majestic images – two of the Buddha, one most probably of his disciple, Ananda – drew our mind into contemplation. On the way back to Colombo, we noticed crowds of people and a host of army personnel at Habarana, a major road junction. Only later did we hear that the day before, just over two hours after we ourselves had passed that spot on our way to Polonnaruwa, three buses had been stopped by Tamil militants and the occupants – men, women and children – killed. The target had been soldiers returning home on leave. We had travelled towards beauty, peace and contemplation but, if we had caught a later bus, could have been caught up in the killing. Others had not been so fortunate.

In Buddhism there is more than one form of *dukkha*. One kind is inherent in the very fact of our birth. If we are born, we are programmed to age and to die, simply because we are human. Life is a death sentence. We cannot prevent this, even if we become enlightened in the course of our life. Most experiences of *dukkha*, however, according to the Buddha's teachings, are created by us. They are not inherent within existence. They arise because they have a cause and this cause, Buddhists would say, lies in the minds and hearts of living beings. It lies in the way we react to all that the world throws at us.

A world shot through with craving

In the Pāli texts, there is a myth of beginnings, the *Aggañña Sutta*,[6] which goes like this. One world implodes and collapses. Some beings from that world are reborn in one of the heavens. In Buddhist cosmology there are both heavens and hells. When another world begins to form, these beings are re-born into the new world. At first, they are not embodied. They are made of mind, and are long-lived and self-luminous. There are no gender differences. Traits in their psyche, however, mean that this situation does not last. The text narrates how these beings gradually gain physical bodies, lose their self-luminosity and their longevity, and divide into male and female, attractive and unattractive, and eventually into different trades and occupations – in other words, become human. The key to this whole development is craving and the growth of individualism. The luminous beings see a tasty, sweet crust on the earth and begin to eat it. They become attached to it. Then, the tasty crust disappears and an edible mushroom arises. Attachment and craving develops further and, because of this, they divide into lovely and unlovely. Creepers and then rice appear. The beings then divide into male and female and thoughts of lust arise. A crucial moment is when one being begins to hoard rice rather than take only what is needed for the day. This leads to stealing and jealousy – and eventually to the election of a king to control immorality through state power.

The discourse ends with a human community similar to the monarchies in the India of the Buddha's time, the fifth century BCE, where governance was needed to keep self-interest under control. It is not dissimilar to society in the twenty-first century. The underlying message is that the world as we know it has taken its form because of greed or craving. It is undergirded by craving, a craving that arises in the mind. It is a simple message but then myths are about simple truths that are at the same time profound. The message of the *Aggañña Sutta* forms what is called the

Second Noble Truth in Buddhism, the second insight into reality – the Noble Truth of Arising. *Dukkha* has a cause, this 'Truth' declares, and it is the presence of craving in our minds and hearts. And the sisters of craving are greed and hatred (*lobha* and *dosa*), all of which are rooted in ignorance or delusion (*avijjā*).

The Pāli texts illustrate this using the image of fire:

Bhikkhus, all is burning. And what, bhikkhus, is the all that is burning? The eye is burning, forms are burning, eye-consciousness is burning, eye-contact is burning, and whatever feeling arises with eye-contact as condition – whether pleasant or painful or neither-pleasant-nor-painful – that too is burning. Burning with what? Burning with the fire of lust, with the fire of hatred, with the fire of delusion; burning with birth, ageing, and death; with sorrow, lamentation, pain displeasure, and despair, I say.[7]

The same is said of the other senses, including the mind, which Buddhists see as a sense. Another graphic description comes from the *Aṅguttara Nikāya* of the Pāli Canon:

Monks, I will teach you the craving that ensnares, that floats along, that is far flung, that clings to one, by which this world is smothered, enveloped, tangled like a ball of thread, covered as with blight, twisted up like a grass rope, so that it does not pass beyond the Constant Round, the Downfall, the Way of Woe, the Ruin . . .[8]

Graphic also is this verse about human beings, attributed to Venerable Rahula, the Buddha's son, who, according to tradition, became a Buddhist monk:

Blinded are beings by their sense desires,
Spread over them like a net; covered are they

By a cloak of craving; by their heedless ways
Caught as a fish in mouth of a net.[9]

Craving (*taṇhā*), in the Theravāda tradition, takes three basic forms: craving for sensual pleasure (*kāma taṇhā*), craving for existence (*bhava taṇhā*), and craving for non-existence (*vibhava taṇhā*). In some discourses, the first of these is sub-divided into six, corresponding to the six senses recognized in Theravāda Buddhism: craving for visible objects, for sounds, for smells, for tastes, for touch and for mental impressions.[10] All forms of craving are seen to be rooted in ignorance or delusion (*avijjā*).

According to this world view, humans are locked in a self-made mental and emotional prison because they have conditioned themselves since birth to move towards that which attracts them and away from that which causes aversion, putting the needs of the self at the centre. It is as though humans have a fatal love affair with greed and hatred.[11] Caroline Brazier, a western Buddhist psychologist, speaks of an addiction to self:

. . . but it should be clear from what we have seen so far that what we are looking at in Buddhist psychology is a psychology of addiction. But to what are we addicted? For most of us, it is an addiction to self. The self we create is the source of security and comfort to which we turn when life gets difficult; and this habitual pattern of refuge is just as persistent and just as falsely based as any substance addiction.[12]

Buddhism offers a series of interdependent, causally related, stages in the arising of *dukkha*. It is an expression of what Buddhism calls conditioned arising or *paṭicca samuppāda*. It begins before birth with ignorance and then passes to what Peter Harvey has called, 'constructing activities' and discriminative consciousness. The mind and body are then formed and the six sense bases. The interaction between the senses and sensory stimulation then produces feeling, which, in turn, produces craving and then grasping. These then fuel existence, birth, ageing, death and sorrow.[13]

It is worth bringing in rebirth here. According to most Buddhists in the world, with Chinese, Japanese and some western Buddhists possible exceptions, and certainly in the texts of Theravāda Buddhism, living beings are repeatedly born into one of several planes of being, including heavens and hells, because they have not rid themselves of greed, hatred and delusion. Their actions in one life, through the Law of Kamma, determine what happens to them after death. Some Buddhists place great emphasis on the thought in the mind at the moment of death. If it is pure, then the moment after death will also be pure, paving the way for a good rebirth. If it is marked by hatred, clinging or fear, then the moment after death will also be so marked, opening the way to a worse rebirth. The majority of Buddhists would agree that if their minds and hearts are still conditioned by the poisons of greed and hatred, they will be reborn to experience *dukkha* again. Another narrative from the Pāli texts illustrates exactly what this means and why the prospect of rebirth after rebirth is so terrifying for the reflective Buddhist. Ubbirī is the daughter of an eminent burgess. She is beautiful and is brought into the house of the King of Kosala, a king contemporary to the Buddha. When she gives birth to a daughter, Jīva (life), she is made queen. However, the daughter dies and Ubbirī repeatedly goes to the cemetery to mourn. One day the Buddha comes to her there and the conversation goes something like this:

The Buddha: Why are you crying?
Ubbirī: I cry because of my daughter, Exalted One.
The Buddha: Cremated in this cemetery are 84,000 of your daughters. Which one are you weeping for?[14]

The time spans with which Buddhist cosmology works are simply mind-shaking. Worlds form and collapse. Mountains are worn down to the plane. And existence goes on, driven by craving.

In the narratives found in the Buddhist texts, craving operates not only at the individual level but also at the institutional level. There is one narrative, in the *Cakkavatti Sīhanāda Sutta* (The Lion-Roar on the Turning of the Wheel) that shows a society falling into anarchy, violence and internecine war. First theft appears because people are poor and they need food to live. Punishment by the state fails to deter this. Murder, lying, adultery, incest and false speech follow. Eventually, what the discourse calls a sword period arises in which people look at one other as if they were wild beasts, take swords and deprive each other of life. What is most interesting about the story is that poverty is not the first cause. The discourse makes it clear that poverty arose because the king did not heed the advice of his spiritual counsellors that wealth should be given to whomsoever is poor. It is from a failure of governance that breakdown arises, springing from greed within the institutions of government to keep wealth to itself. It is this that then conditions the minds of those who turn to violence in order to survive.[15]

People who are not Buddhist may find the concept of birth and rebirth, on the scale depicted in the Buddhist texts, difficult to accept. What Buddhism has to say about the human condition, however, is not dependent on this. Even with rebirth edited out, the view of the world that I have outlined so far may appear fairly dark to the outsider. When evangelical Christian missionaries encountered it in the nineteenth century, in countries such as Burma and Sri Lanka, some were horrified. For instance, Wesleyan missionary, Thomas Moscrop, who served in Sri Lanka between 1883 and 1900, wrote this:

Buddhism – a religion without God and without hope in the world – is too pessimistic, too cold, too antagonistic to the constitution of human nature to take the world captive. Buddhism cannot succeed for it says, 'There is no good, but all is evil in human existence'.[16]

Presbyterian missionary John Murdoch (1819–1904), who worked in Sri Lanka and India for almost 60 years, wrote this in a pamphlet addressed to educated Buddhists to show them, as he saw it, the error of their beliefs:

> As a devout Buddhist counts his beads, he mutters *Anitya, Dukha, Anatta*, 'Transience, Sorrow, Unreality'. Existence is a curse, and the greatest aim should be annihilation or nothingness.[17]

Conditioned by the optimism present at the height of Victorian England, which included the conviction that God had ordained Britain to bring Christianity to the world in a civilizing and humanizing mission, Christians such as Moscrop and Murdoch asked themselves, 'Why would anyone want to subscribe to such a religion?' If they had lived at the beginning of the twenty-first century, post-European imperialism, post the modernism that placed implicit trust in science, their reaction may have been different. Global warming, the inequities in world trade and the number of internal wars in the world are making more people aware of how greed functions in the world and also that religion itself has a dark side.

In a piece I wrote for a Sri Lankan feminist magazine, this is how I voiced my own reaction to the Buddhist world view:

> ... Buddhism's view of human society as enmeshed in selfish craving, torn between greed and hatred, seeing the permanent in what is impermanent, makes sense to me. I look at Sri Lanka, England and many other countries where there are conflicts and injustices and see the causes of these just where the Buddha located them. I see greed institutionalised in many

expressions of capitalism and, in ethno-nationalistic wars, I see what Buddhism would call 'clinging to views and opinions', namely clinging inflexibly to one position with a 'this alone is truth' mentality. Buddhism's view of the world is dark, but nevertheless realistic.[18]

When I first encountered Buddhism, the view of the world it offered simply made sense to me. It made me more aware of the subtle ways in which the world is dominated by greed – individual, corporate and institutional – and the different kinds of greed that come into play, many of which are spoken of in the Buddhist texts, whether it is clinging to views and opinions (*diṭṭhi* – thinking my views alone can be right and everyone else's wrong) or forever weighing oneself against others (*māna*) to affirm one's own superiority. Our greed is ruining the environment, not only individual greed but national and institutional greed. Our greed has now made us the victim. And when I consider the three forms of craving, even craving for non-existence becomes significant, for it is the kind of craving that will say, 'We need not take responsibility for the future of the earth. We have one life and we will soon be dead. Let us enjoy our lives while we can. Let us not worry about the future.' Global warming, for instance, need not be thought about nor the possibility that nuclear weapons will be used.

In reply to the missionary accusation that the Buddhist view of the world is pessimistic, I and many Buddhists would, therefore, reply, 'No, it's realistic. It represents how things are in our world today.' It is a realistic lens through which to see the powers that are currently dominant in the world and have been throughout history. Humans may have an altruistic gene but they also have a greedy one.

As for Murdoch's view that Buddhists view existence as a curse, he was, quite frankly, wrong. For Buddhists of all schools, human birth is incredibly precious and it is hard won. There are many other planes that a living being can be born into. Theravāda Buddhism speaks of five: the heavens, the human realm, the plane of the hungry ghosts, the animal realm and the hell realms. Mahāyāna Buddhism adds one more – the plane of the *asuras* or demigods, just below those of the gods (the heavens). Not one of these is permanent and, of all of them, a human existence is considered to be the best in terms of spiritual potential. There is one image in the Theravāda Canon that shows just how hard a human birth is once a being has fallen to one of the hells. The Buddha is speaking to his monks and asks them to visualize a man who might throw a yoke with one hole into the sea. It is blown by the wind, westwards, eastwards, southwards and north-wards. There is a blind turtle who comes to the surface every 100 years. It would be more difficult, the Buddha declares, for a being in 'the Downfall' to gain a human birth than for that turtle to come up through the hole in the ring.[19] As one Dhammapada verse put it, 'It is difficult to obtain birth as a human.'[20] Buddhists in the Tibetan tradition begin a period of meditation in recollec-tion of four things that turn the mind to meditation practice, the first of which is, 'How joyful to find such a human birth, difficult to find, free and well-favoured.'[21]

A human life is precious for two main reasons. The first is that Buddhism does not end with the view that living beings are imprisoned in greed, hatred and delusion. It asserts that there is a way out of this prison. The second is that a human birth is the best birth within which to work towards this release.

Liberation is possible

The Buddha's message was that *dukkha* and that which fuels it – greed, hatred and delusion – can be overcome, through trans-forming the way we look at the world and through transforming the mind and the heart through plucking out greed, hatred and delusion. This is linked in Buddhism with the Law of Kamma

(Sanskrit: *Karma*), the law that asserts that each action has a fruit. Wholesome or good actions will bear wholesome, good fruit. Unwholesome or evil actions will bear unwholesome, evil fruit. Significantly, volition, the will to do something, is also considered as 'action'. So, for instance, the intention to murder someone will bear fruit, even if the action is never carried out. All this is undergirded by the Law of Cause and Effect, which is central to Buddhism. If we do evil, if we are driven by our greed and hatred, then the fruit will be negative. If we do good, the fruit cannot but be positive. So the first pair of verses in the Dhammapada include these phrases:

If one speaks or acts with an evil mind, from that sorrow follows him, as the wheel follows the foot of the ox.

If one speaks and acts with a pure mind, from that happiness follows him, like a shadow not going away,[22]

So when this Law is applied to the experience of *dukkha*, we reach this: if the cause of *dukkha* is eradicated, *dukkha* is eradicated. If craving – and the greed, hatred and ignorance connected with it – is eradicated, *dukkha* cannot arise. We can be liberated from it. At any moment, a person can begin to change his or her life by transforming the way he or she relates to the world. In contrast to the missionaries in the nineteenth century, there were other westerners, at the same time, who saw this as Buddhism's supreme message. Edwin Arnold, for instance, in his 1879 popular poem on the life and teaching of the Buddha, *The Light of Asia*, openly contested the missionary view:

If ye lay bound upon the wheel of change,
And no way were of breaking from the chain,
The Heart of boundless Being is a curse,
The Soul of Things fell Pain.

Ye are not bound! the Soul of Things is sweet,
The Heart of Being is celestial rest;
Stronger than woe is will; that which is Good
Doth pass to Better – Best.[23]

To pass to the second reason for the preciousness of human birth, Buddhists would say that the human plane has just the right balance of joy and pain for humans to recognize that there is a problem with existence and to do something about it. In the hells, the pains are too great for this to happen and in the heavens the pleasures are too sublime. As a human there is both pain and pleasure, usually in equal measure. Both heaven and hell are experienced and the contrast between the two is the teacher or the prompter.

Another conversation with Sr Nyanasiri is relevant here. We were again speaking about the political turmoil in Sri Lanka. Although deploring the level of violence, Nyanasiri said that there was one positive outcome. Some of the middle-class Buddhists that she encountered were asking more questions about Buddhism, because they were beginning to see what *dukkha* was all about. Poverty had not touched them, since most were from privileged or at least comfortable backgrounds. They had not lost children because of illness because they could afford medical bills. They were happily married. The ethnic conflict had not affected them directly. But the JVP was a different matter. Hardly one family in Kandy was free from fear, either that the military would kill a relation because he had been to a JVP meeting or that the JVP itself would find a traitor in their family. The experience of *dukkha* was a reality. And they wanted to know how to cope with it. They were no longer content with a Buddhism that remained at the level of *sīla* (morality) and devotion – observing the five ethical precepts and eight on Full Moon Days, lighting lamps and offering flowers at the *vihāra*, being present at Pirit recitals, giving food to members of the monastic Sangha. They sought mental peace and strength, the task of meditation.

That there is a way out of *dukkha* is pictorially illustrated in much Buddhist art, most famously in the well-known wheel of life in the Tibetan Buddhist tradition. It hangs in most Tibetan Buddhist centres, a massive sphere in a large squarish frame. Tibetan tradition says that it was first created for the King of Magadha (one of the kings in the time of the Buddha), under the Buddha's instruction. This is the description of it that was given to me, in 1995, by Ringu Tulku, a revered Tibetan teacher, now resident in Bhutan, during interviews that I conducted for a series of radio programmes that I wrote and presented for the BBC World Service series in 1995/6: *The Way of the Buddha*. It sums up much of what I have explained so far.

The most important thing is in the centre where there are three animals, intermingled, each holding the tale of the other – a snake, a pig and a bird. These three animals represent the three basic conflicting or afflictive emotions. The pig represents ignorance, not knowing, not understanding the way things are, not knowing who you are. And from there come two things, aversion and attachment. The snake represents aversion, anger, short-temperedness. Then, the bird or cock represents attachment or desire. Because of our ignorance, we react to things either with aversion or attachment. These three things are the cause, the seed, of the whole *samsaric* state of mind. That is why they are in the centre.

Then, around that, are pictures in a circle. Half of the circle is white and half is black. In the white part, you can see some people going up, led by a *lama*. Then, on the other side, there is a black strip, where people are going down, head first. This indicates cause and effect related to action, *karma*. If you do positive deeds then you go up, in the light. If you do negative things, you go down, towards darkness. Then, around that, there's a bigger circle divided into six sections in which the six realms are depicted. At the top is the gods realm. Next to it is the demi-gods realm (*asuras*). To the left of it is the human realm. Then below, at the bottom, is the hell realm. To the right is the realm of the hungry ghosts. And to the left is the animal realm. Now, these six realms represent the result of our six kinds of emotions. The god's realm represents the emotion of pride; the demi-gods, jealousy; the human realm, desire; the animal realm, dullness; the hungry ghost realm, stinginess, miserliness and the hell realm, hatred and anger. The six realms are the whole of the *samsaric* state of mind. They depict the whole of *saṃsāra*. Wherever you go in these six realms there's no complete peace, no complete happiness. It's always covered, overpowered, by greed, hatred and illusion.

Then around that there's another smaller circle, with twelve pictures in twelve small sections, which represent the twelve dependent originations which illustrate how we get reborn again and again. They show the process through which we move through the *samsaric* world, the wheel of life, being born again and again. It starts with ignorance, which is depicted as an old person, who is blind. The second picture is of someone who is making pottery. That represents concepts. Because of our ignorance, because we do not know we are conscious, we make lots of concepts. These two together then give rise to the whole thing. The chain then covers name and form – our physical body – and then the six senses. Six senses develop into contact with objects and when we have contact with objects through the six senses, sensation arises. Then, when we have feeling, we have grasping, attachment to it. Then, if it is a nice sensation and we like it, we become attached to it and if it is not so nice we feel aversion, we are afraid of it. This fear and attachment create *karma*. When this *karma* ripens through grasping it is what we call becoming. There is no other possibility but to become – to take the next stage. If it is a rebirth, then the next rebirth. If it is a momentary thing, then the next moment of the *samsaric* mind. Then there is the depiction of a child being born, representing birth. Then you have old age and death. Once we are born, there is no other way but to go on to old age and death. It then again starts with ignorance for we go on and on as in a circle.

The whole thing is carried by a wrathful-looking, ferocious person, who is eating it up in his mouth. That represents time, Yama-raja, the Lord of Death, which is impermanence. So the whole of this cycle of life is impermanent. It is eaten up by the Lord of Death all the time. Then, out in one corner, you can see a Buddha pointing towards the sky. This shows there is a way out of the *samsaric* state of mind. The Buddha who shattered the chain of dependent origination got rid of the *karma* and fled the *samsaric* chain of action and reaction. So that is freedom, *nirvāṇa*. Then there is also a small stanza in Tibetan saying the same thing in verse.[24]

The Buddha is there in the corner. It is almost possible to miss him, the perspective of the picture is so overwhelmingly weighted on the side of the forces that keep us within the round of birth and rebirth. In Buddhist temples throughout the world, however, the Buddha is central. No chapter on what Buddhism says about the human condition can be complete without returning to the Buddha. The world view of Buddhism is not pessimistic because Buddhists believe the light of the Buddha and his teachings shines into each era and into every corner of the cosmos for those with eyes to see.

The Venerable Ananda Metteyya (the second British person to become a Buddhist monk), whom I've quoted before, wrote this of the Burmese people:

There, into the daily lives, the very speech and household customs of the common folk, this ever-present sun-light of the Teaching penetrated; there, hearing at a fiesta the gathered crowds take refuge in the Buddha, you could all but see them turn their faces to bathe them in the splendour of His very presence – till one could understand how, instead of getting angry when they hear the Christian missionaries tell them they are taking refuge in a Being whom their own religion tells them has utterly passed away, they always answer, as they do answer, only with a wise and a compassionate smile.[25]

I can understand that compassionate and wise look. Theravāda Buddhists believe that each era produces one Buddha, one being who, through numerous lives, masters ten perfections, including liberality, morality, renunciation and loving-kindness, in preparation for a final life as a Buddha. When that Buddha – Siddhartha Gotama, for this era – awakes to liberating Truth, he becomes more than human. He becomes 'a wonderful man', 'a teacher of gods and humans', 'a knower of worlds', to quote some phrases that the texts use of such a person. He becomes the embodiment of the teaching, the embodiment of compassion and wisdom, the two poles of enlightenment in Buddhism. Theravāda Buddhists use the following salutation:

Such, indeed is the blessed One: Exalted, Omniscient, Endowed with knowledge and virtue, Auspicious, Knower of Worlds, A Guide incomparable for the training of individuals; Teacher of gods and humans, Enlightened and Holy.

The Mahāyāna tradition went beyond the Theravāda tradition in its representation of what Buddhahood was. Not content with the view that there is only one Buddha in every era, they came to believe that Buddhas are as numerous as the sands on the river Ganges and could exist simultaneously. The historical Buddha, Siddhartha Gautama, was eventually seen as an embodiment of the cosmic reality of Buddhahood. Most Mahāyāna schools also stress that each person, because of innate buddha nature, can become a Buddha by following the compassionate path of a Buddha-to-be, a *bodhisattva* (Pāli: *bodhisatta*). Added to this were numerous celestial *bodhisattvas*, beings who had taken a vow not to enter *nirvāṇa* until all living beings have been liberated and whose sole vocation is to help living beings attain *nirvāṇa*.

It is for reasons such as these that the Buddha image is a focal point for intense devotion, which includes prostration, chanting and the offering of flowers, light and incense. As devotees position themselves in front of the image, they imagine the Buddha's compassion and wisdom. For some, these qualities come alive, flowing from the image, bathing them in light. It was this that I glimpsed in my first encounter with the Buddha at Anuradhapura. I have sensed it many times since.

So any account of the Buddhist view of the human condition must include the fact that we are not alone in the cosmos, trapped by our ignorance and our craving. Humanity has the Buddhas as guides and inspiration, embodiments of the compassion and wisdom that Buddhists are convinced lie at the heart of the cosmos. These show the path to liberation and this will be the topic of the next chapter.

Notes

1 *Saṃyutta Nikāya*, text IV 136, F. L. Woodward (trans.), 1980, *The Book of Kindred Sayings*, Book IV, Oxford: Pāli Text Society, p. 82.

2 Dhammapada, verse 174, K. R. Norman (trans.), 1997, *The Word of the Doctrine* (Dhammapada), Oxford: Pāli Text Society, p. 26.

3 Scholars such as Richard Gombrich and Heinz Bechert have argued that the Buddha lived in the fifth century BCE, not the sixth as in some traditional histories. See Lance S. Cousins, 1996, 'The Dating of the Historical Buddha: A Review Article', *Journal of the Royal Asiatic Society*, Series 3, 6.1, pp. 57–63.

4 Buddhist scholar, Peter Harvey, has argued that the Four Noble Truths are not ontological Truths but realities of existence that the Buddha preached to those who had ears to hear (unpublished research).

5 *Aṅguttara Nikāya*, text I 26, F. L. Woodward (trans.), *The Book of the Gradual Sayings*, vol. I, Oxford: Pāli Text Society, p. 25.

6 *Aggañña Sutta, Dīgha Nikāya* III, pp. 80–98.

7 From the *Saḷāyatanasaṃyutta, Saṃyutta Nikāya*, Book IV Division I: 28, Bhikkhu Bodhi (trans.) 2000, *The Connected Discourse of the Buddha*, Boston: Wisdom Publications, p. 1143.

8 *Aṅguttara Nikāya*, II 211, F. L. Woodward (trans.), 1992, *The Book of the Gradual Sayings (Aṅguttara Nikāya)*, vol. II, Oxford, Pāli Text Society, p. 225.

9 Verse ascribed to Rāhula, *Psalms of the Early Buddhists: Verses of the Brethren*, Caroline Rhys Davids (trans.), Oxford: Pāli Text Society, 1913, p. 183.

10 See for example *Sammādiṭṭhi Sutta, Majjhima Nikāya*, Vol. I, p. 51.

11 See Harris, 2002, 'The Beginning of Something Being Broken', p. 16.

12 Caroline Brazier, 2003, *Buddhist Psychology: Liberate Your Mind, Embrace Life*, London: Robinson, p. 33.

13 See Peter Harvey, 1990, *An Introduction to Buddhism: Teachings, History and Practices*, Cambridge: Cambridge University Press, p. 54.

14 The story connected with the verses of Ubbiri in the *Therīgāthā* (Verses of the Sisters), vv. 51–3.

15 *Cakkavatti Sīhanāda Sutta, Dīgha Nikāya*, vol. III, pp. 58–79.

16 Thomas Moscrop, 1889, *Christ and the Buddha Historically Compared*, Colombo: Ceylon Religious Tract Soceity, p. 95, quoted in Harris, 2006, *Theravāda Buddhism and the British Encounter*, p. 104.

17 J. Murdoch, 1887, *Buddha and his Religion – Compiled from the Works of Gogerly, Bigandet, Kellogg, Titcomb, Davids, Oldenburg and others*, India: Christian Vernacular Education Society, pp. 22–34, quoted in Harris, 2006, *Theravāda Buddhism and the British Encounter*, p. 105.

18 Elizabeth J. Harris, 'Why have anything to do with religion?' in *Options* vol. 23, no. 3, 2000, pp. 21–2.

19 *Bālapaṇḍita Sutta, Majjhima Nikāya*, vol. III 169, I. B. Horner (trans.), 1990, *The Middle Length Sayings*, Oxford: Pāli Text Society, p. 215.

20 Dhammapada, v. 182.

21 Ramona Kauth and Elizabeth J. Harris (eds), 2004, *Meeting Buddhists*, Leicester: Christians Aware, pp. 299–330.

22 Dhammapada, vv. 1 and 2, K. R. Norman (trans.), *The Word of the Doctrine (Dhammapada)*, p. 1.

23 Edwin Arnold, 1879 (1906), *The Light of Asia or the Great Renunciation Being the Life and Teaching of Gautama Prince of India and Founder of Buddhism*, London: Kegan Paul, Trench, Trubner & Co. Ltd, pp. 141–2.

24 Reprinted in: Elizabeth J. Harris, 1998, *What Buddhists Believe*, Oxford: Oneworld, pp. 46–7.

25 Harris, 1998, *Ananda Metteyya*, pp. 27–8.

3

The Path

Bishop Tom Butler's 'Thought for the Day' after the Virginia Tec killings did not end with the scream of anguish present in Munch's work of art but with a plea for action, for human care. As the last chapter has shown, Buddhism also does not end with the awareness that our world is shot through with greed and hatred. It calls people to a path of action to uproot greed and hatred, the causes of suffering and pain. It affirms that change is possible. And this possibility for change throws a positive light around the characteristics of human existence. As Professor Lily de Silva, university teacher of Buddhism and Pāli, once said to me when explaining the concept of *anattā* (non-self), 'If there is one part of the human person that cannot change, then *nibbāna* would not be possible.'

One narrative from the texts stands out for me when I think of the Buddhist path. It concerns a Buddhist monk, a *bhikkhu*, named Malunkyaputta, who approaches the Buddha and accuses him of not answering some of the most important questions about human life: Is the world eternal or finite? Is the soul different from the body or is it the same? Does a Buddha exist after death or not? He threatens to abandon the Buddha's teachings and become a lay person again if the Buddha does not give him answers. The Buddha then replies, 'Did I ever say to you, "Come Malunkyaputta, lead the holy life with me and I will answer all these questions"?' The *bhikkhu* has to admit that the Buddha did not. The Buddha then tells a parable, in which the central character is compared to Malunkyaputta. Imagine a man wounded with an arrow, thickly smeared with poison. His friends bring a surgeon to treat him, but the wounded man refuses to have the arrow extracted. Before he will allow this to happen, he insists, he must know the answer to certain questions: Was the person who shot him a noble, a merchant or a worker? Was this man tall or short or of middle height? Was he dark or brown or golden skinned? Which village, town or city did he live in? Was the bow that wounded him a long bow or a crossbow? Was the bowstring made of reed, sinew, hemp or bark? Was the shaft that wounded him wild or cultivated? Were the feathers of the shaft those of a vulture, crow, hawk, peacock or stork? Was the sinew with which the shaft was bound that of an ox, a buffalo, a lion or a monkey? Was the arrow hoof-tipped, curved, barbed or calf-toothed?

The questions seem endless and Malunkyaputta would have been left in no doubt that the man would have died before all these questions could have been answered. So too, the Buddha points out, will the person who refuses to follow the holy life under the Buddha until he knows the answers to what Buddhism now calls 'the unanswered questions'. The message of the 'parable' is clear. The need of the moment for the injured person was for the poisoned arrow to be extracted to prevent death, not the search for answers to questions that were peripheral to whether the person would live or die. Similarly, the task for Malunkyaputta was to extract the poisons in his own mind and body, not to speculate on whether the world was eternal or not.[1]

The task: plucking out greed, hatred and delusion

Buddhists use this narrative to throw light on the task for all human beings. We all have poison inside us, Buddhism insists, the poisons of greed, hatred and delusion. These must be extracted if wholeness, liberation, freedom from *dukkha* are to arise. Metaphysical questions that do not relate to this goal are irrelevant. Wholeness and liberation is called *nibbāna* (Pāli) or *nirvāṇa* (Sanskrit) by Buddhists. Ideally, everything within the Buddhist path is subordinated to it. The texts are economical in what they say about *nirvāṇa*. It is a state that arises when the poisons of greed, hatred and delusion have been eradicated from the heart and mind. It is liberation from the prison of self and liberation from rebirth. As such, it is the highest bliss, the highest happiness and the highest truth. Professor Y. Karunadasa, one of my teachers, also used to stress that it is the highest ethical good – the 'good' that arises when greed and hatred are no more and the enlightened person has become compassion and wisdom embodied. Mahāyāna Buddhists picture it as the realization of our inherent, pure Buddha Nature. Some Buddhists will insist that *nibbāna* is possible in this very life; others, most probably the majority in Asia, will say that many lives will be needed before it is attained and that all the ordinary person can aspire to is a rebirth in one of the heavens.

A path of withdrawal or engagement

How is this task of extracting poison to be carried out? What do Buddhists have to do? What path do they need to follow? These were among the most important questions for me in my first year in Sri Lanka. Since one of the concerns I had brought to my encounter was whether Buddhism had resources that would aid campaigns for social justice in the world, I was particularly interested in whether the eradication of greed and hatred had anything to do with social action. I knew that one western stereotype of Buddhism was that it was only concerned with withdrawal and an individualistic form of meditation, but I could not believe this to be the whole story. I did not feel the same way as one Christian missionary colleague who, in the 1980s, said to me, 'The Buddha image speaks to me of coldness, of non-involvement, of a turning away from life. I prefer the image of Jesus Christ with his robes dirty with the sweat of the poor.'[2]

Some of my first meditation teachers, however, seemed to play into the individualistic stereotype by stressing that the only world we need to be concerned about is the world inside ourselves and that our only goal should be finding a transcendent happiness untouched by the imperfections of our world. 'Since there is nothing else really worth attending to, let us attend to our own body and mind,' I read in a booklet written by Venerable Ayya Khema, an organizer of the women's conference at Bodh Gaya mentioned in the first chapter and one of my first teachers of meditation. The booklet made a distinction between self-image and self-knowledge and urged its readers to embark on the mental culture that would help us drop our ego-driven self-image.[3] Was this where Buddhism and Christianity diverged, I wondered?

At a meditation day I attended with Venerable Khema, then Sr Khema, she voiced something similar, by saying that the second *jhāna* (meditative absorption) could provide us with a state of happiness to which we could always return so that life, with its difficulties, could not touch us so much. I can remember saying out loud, 'My problem is with the suffering of others. I ask myself whether I want to be untouched by their suffering.' She answered, with some disdain, 'A very Christian comment. If one suffers with those who suffer, there are two people suffering instead of one and that does not help the situation. What help is given, if one cries with the person who is crying? But we can show compassion, and, as far as our insight goes, point to the way out of suffering. How far we can do this will depend on our own point on the path and how far we have released ourselves from suffering. We should strive to help and not just be a do-gooder.'

I wanted to continue the conversation for I had spoken about being touched by suffering, not suffering together with those who suffer. There was a subtle difference between the two, I felt. I restrained myself. Not to have done so would have broken the

61

teacher–learner relationship, as I had found to my discredit at a session with another meditation teacher, when I had suggested that a point I had made had been misunderstood, whereupon the teacher had said to the whole group, 'The process of sharing is not for argument.'

Sr Khema was not advocating complete withdrawal from society, far from it, but was suggesting that work on self must come before one could offer effective help to others. I encountered something similar in other meditation sessions. For instance, in one, the *bhikkhu* leading the session had opened by saying, 'Do you want the world to change?' My initial reaction was, 'Of course I want it to change – to change for the better.' The reaction the *bhikkhu* sought, however, was different. He wanted us to respond, 'No, I'm content with things as they are. I do not need to seek for ever more pleasurable experiences or an ever more exalted status in society.' His focus was the mind and its ego-driven tendencies, not peace and justice issues.

These two meditation teachers were voicing an important side of Theravāda Buddhism. There is no doubt that Buddhism speaks about a personal task that only we ourselves can undertake, that of rooting out from the mind, greed, hatred and delusion. In the Theravāda tradition, the last recorded words of the Buddha are, 'Strive on untiringly' or 'Accomplish earnestly'.[4] I came to realize both that there was no easy answer to whether this earnestness meant withdrawal or active engagement with society and that the question was not simply mine, as an outsider, but was also one that caused divisions within the Buddhist community.

On one hand, I found that there was definitely an undercurrent in Sri Lankan culture that went much further than either of the two meditation teachers I have mentioned in fascination for the one who could remain untouched, aloof and detached from life. In the mid-1980s, a film of a novel by Martin Wickramasinghe[5] was released in Sri Lanka. Called *Viragaya* (nonattachment), it was about Arvinda, an intensely introverted man, who is unable to relate to anything or anyone with enthusiasm. Instead of studying for his exams in medicine, the young man writes a diary of his own thoughts. He is kind, compassionate and unthinking of self. When a girl richer than he falls in love with him, he does not grasp her love or truly respond to it, although he is fond of her. She is married to someone else, with greater wealth. When his father dies, his sister makes it impossible for either he or his mother to live in the family home. So he rents a room, in a house owned by a woman with a daughter. He tutors the daughter who eventually calls him father. When the girl is older, though, rumours go round that there is something improper in the relationship. Arvinda is ostracized. He becomes ill and dies a lonely man. Only after his death, do people become interested in Arvinda the thinker, the philosopher. Arvinda, I came to realize, expressed an ever present urge or ideal in a Buddhist society like Sri Lanka – the ability simply to 'be', without 'having', to live without anger, sensual involvement, bitterness or slander and to be able to renounce passion and possessions.

Whether the Buddhist path concerned an individualistic practice to gain personal liberation or one that embraced all living beings in activist compassion was one of the issues surrounding the arising of what is now known as Mahāyāna Buddhism (The Great Way). Mahāyāna Buddhism evolved in India between the first century BCE and the early centuries CE, most probably within the monasteries. It built on what had gone before but developed what Paul Williams has called, 'a particular vision of what the final motivation and goal of serious practitioners should be'.[6] That vision included a condemnation of earlier schools because they were judged to be too individualistic, too Arvinda-like. They belonged to *Hinayāna* – the lesser way. Far better was the Way that placed compassion for all living beings at the centre.

Lives of generosity, loving kindness and self-sacrifice

One important point about Wickramasinghe's novel, however, was that Arvinda was an exception, avoided by the villagers during his life, although the subject of fascination after his death. Buddhism as practised by villagers in the Theravāda Buddhist communities of Sri Lanka has never been about withdrawal from social involvement. It has never been the *Hinayāna* of Mahāyāna polemic. A traditional Buddhist triad, *dāna, sīla, bhāvanā* (generosity, morality or virtue, and meditation) has governed their lives and still does. The first, *dāna*, means, above all, generosity to the monastic community, in other words providing the *bhikkhus* and the ten precept contemporary nuns (*dasa sil māthās*) in the village with their physical needs. But it is not restricted to this. It spills out into an attitude of generosity for all. *Sīla*, morality, is governed by what are known as the five precepts, which are voluntarily undertaken moral commitments that go back to the beginnings of Buddhism: not to harm any living being; not to take anything that is not given; not to be involved in sexual or sensual misconduct; not to say anything that is false; and not to ingest intoxicants that cloud the mind, such as alcohol or hallucinogenic drugs. Whenever Buddhists go to a *vihāra* and sit at the feet of *bhikkhus* or *dasa sil māthās* for teaching, they recite or 'take' the five precepts, in Pāli, and, once taken, they are not broken, at least for the day on which they are taken. A Buddhist woman friend told me a traditional story to illustrate the binding nature of this. A man finds that a snake is winding itself around his body, gradually crushing his internal organs. He is tempted to kill the snake, but remembers that he has taken the five precepts. He refrains and is squeezed to death.

Behind the precepts is an argument for morality through empathy. Most Buddhists, even those who do not know many texts at all, would know these verses from the Dhammapada:

All tremble at violence; all fear death. Comparing (others) with oneself, one should not kill or cause to kill.

All tremble at violence; to all life is dear. Comparing (others) with oneself, one should not kill or cause to kill.[7]

Although couched in a vocabulary of refraining, of withdrawing from, the precepts also imply the pro-active. Each has a positive corollary. If one is to be successful in not harming any living being, then one has to develop loving kindness and compassion. If one is to successfully refrain from taking what is not given, then one has to respect the rights of 'the other' to land, to shelter, to security. If one is to master refraining from false speech, then one has to develop respect and tolerance.

These positives are linked with another task that is central to the Buddhist path: developing the opposites of greed, hatred and delusion. Four qualities are particularly praised – loving kindness (*mettā*); compassion (*karuṇā*); sympathetic joy (*muditā* – being able to take joy in the success of another even though one is not experiencing success oneself); equanimity (*upekkhā* – being able to think and act without being torn between greed and hatred). They are called divine abidings (*brahmavihāras*) and are known by all Buddhists, from the most unsophisticated to the most sophisticated. An ancient discourse on the first of them, *mettā*, has these words at its heart: 'Just as a mother would protect her child at the risk of her own life, so cultivate a boundless heart (of loving kindness) to all beings.'[8] This includes surrounding your enemies or those you do not like with loving kindness.

It is most significant that, in the triad, *dāna*, *sīla*, *bhāvanā*, generosity and virtue come before meditation. They are the bedrock on which meditation must rest. They are also 'meritorious', to use a westernized phrase. In other words, Buddhists know they will bear good fruit according to the Law of *Kamma*. In addition to the five precepts, in traditional Sri Lankan Buddhism, there are also ten good deeds (*dasa kusala kamma* lit.: ten wholesome actions). They begin with the *dāna*, *sīla*, and *bhāvanā*, and then continue with: transferring merit (for example transferring the merit made through wholesome acts to the dead, who, if they are in the lower worlds, are believed not to be able to make merit for themselves); rejoicing in another's merit; performance of religious obligations; paying homage, usually to elders and members of the monastic Sangha; preaching and becoming *kalyāṇamittas* to others (good friends who help others to know the *Dhamma*); listening to preaching; right belief.[9] These emphasize care for one's own well-being, devotion, the cultivation of a compassionate mind that rejoices when others do well and the wish to aid beings in planes less conducive to spiritual progress. In other words, they combine care for self and care for others. In both urban and rural areas in countries such as Sri Lanka, they still form the bedrock of religious practice for the majority of Buddhists. And the spirit behind them accords well with the message of the Pāli texts. For instance, one discourse in the Theravāda Canon shows the Buddha speaking to his son, Rahula, who was then a monk, about how he should decide between different courses of action. The criteria he gives is that any deed of body, speech or mind should be discouraged if it conduces to the harm of self, the harm of others or the harm of both self and others.[10] This is a basic principle of Buddhism. Harm of self and harm of others is intimately connected. If one harms others, one, in fact, harms self.

One of the nineteenth-century British civil servants who praised this side of village society was Sir Frederick Dickson, who served in Sri Lanka between 1859 and 1885. Contesting the missionaries who accused village Buddhists of amalgamating creeds and practising rituals that were debased, he wrote that Buddhism, 'lives enshrined in the hearts of a pious, simple, kindly people; it leads them through a life of charity to a peaceful deathbed such as most Christians may envy'.[11]

It was in the villages that I also found voices that complemented the meditation teachers I mentioned at the beginning of this chapter. For instance, when I was staying with Fr Michael Rodrigo's community at 'Good Wishes House', described further in Chapter 6, I visited Tibbotuwawa Vihāra, in a rural village in the south of the country, where I met the Venerable Alutwela Upananda. Tibbotuwawa Vihāra was an ancient monastery, reached by a long track that wound through rice (paddy) fields. The first *vihāra* on the spot had been built between 9 and 21 CE. Father Mike and I could not spend long with him. Although it was only about 10.00 a.m., he already had to walk to his *dāna*, to the place where lay people would give him, and probably other monks, his main meal of the day, which had to be taken before midday. So we strode back through the paddy fields together. Knowing we were Christian, Ven. Upananda said at one point, 'Self-sacrifice for others, not for oneself, is what binds together different faiths.' He went on to say that part of his sacrifice was to live in an isolated temple such as Tibbotuwawa Vihāra, where the villagers were scattered and poor. That people would give him food every day was not guaranteed. There was deep concern and compassion for the people in his words. He knew their difficulties intimately, for example that the majority of them were indebted for at least half of the year. Their hunger, at times, would have led to his. 'A monk committed to human rights for the people; a monk willing to work for the rights of the people,' Fr Mike later said to me.

In Ven. Alutwela Upananda I found a Buddhist who was not untouched by the suffering of others, and who was expressing this with his life. To a Christian, 'self-sacrifice' might seem a more Christian concept than a Buddhist one. But it is not, although, in Buddhism, it is couched in a vocabulary of gifting and generosity. The gifting of one's body or one's body parts for the good of others is enshrined in Buddhist narrative. The Buddha, when he was a Buddha-to-be or *bodhisatta*, is believed to have gifted himself numerous times in his preparation for his final life when he became Buddha. Five hundred and fifty stories said to be connected with these previous lives are found in a canonical book, called the *Jātaka*. Some of these are taken from a stock of Indian legends; some are very clearly Buddhist. Many of them show the Buddha-to-be demonstrating one or more of ten perfections (*pāramittā*), which include generosity. This is one of them. The Buddha-to-be is a prince called Mahasattva. He and three other princes come across a tiger that is dying of hunger, after giving birth to seven cubs. Mahasattva decides to give his body to the tigress, as a supreme act of generosity and compassion. He asks to be left alone and then throws himself in front of the animal. But she is too weak to kill him and does not move. So he cuts his throat with a sharp piece of bamboo and falls down near the tigress, who then notices his body covered with blood and eats him up.

Even children know such stories, including a more controversial one in which a prince named Vessantara gives away his wife and children to demonstrate non-attachment. Lying behind these narratives is the very Buddhist idea that the path to liberation involves letting go of any clinging to self, letting go of the 'I' and the 'mine'. The most difficult hindrance that has to be overcome before liberation is attained, according to the texts, is the 'I' and 'mine'.

Venerable Upananda's words drew on this tradition, I'm sure. His role was to give himself selflessly for the people around him. Since 1987, I have met other *bhikkhus* like him. Some of them chose to live in the north of the country, in predominantly Tamil areas, at a time when the ethnic conflict was developing. One, the Venerable Delgalle Padumasiri, said to me that he had faced death four times but had never known the fear of death. Another, the Venerable Vavuniya Wimalasara, explained:

When the security forces are exposed to attack and suffer casualties, there are often reprisals against civilians. At such times, the people are defenceless. Here, I have also been in a position to save people. Once, when 16 people were being attacked by a militant group of thugs, I was able to intervene and save their lives.[12]

The way to Nibbāna lies through the pathways of society

One of the favourite sayings of Professor Jotiya Dhirasekera, now the Venerable Dhammavihari, one of my first teachers at the Post-graduate Institute of Pāli and Buddhist Studies, was, 'The way to *nibbāna* lies through the pathways of society.' These monks lived up to this. They were also no doubt inspired by the example of the Buddha and his followers in the Pāli Canon. I shall return to the question of violence later in the book but there is one textual narrative I must quote here. It is the story of the Venerable Punna, who tells the Buddha that he wants to teach in a district where the people are known to be hostile. The Buddha then asks him how he will react if he is attacked. Different possibilities are mentioned, increasing in intensity. Each time, Punna declares that he would be thankful that the abuse was not more serious. But then the Buddha comes to the possibility of death and Punna replies:

If the people of Sunaparanta (possibly Myanmar) deprive me of life with a sharp knife, revered sir, it will be thus for me there: I will say, 'There are disciples of the Lord who, disgusted by the body and the life-principle and ashamed of them, look about for a knife. I have come to this knife without having looked for it.'[13]

Scattered throughout the Pāli Canon are discourses that show the Buddha challenging people to more relevant and appropriate action in society. Many of the discourses are to monks and nuns, but not all. Let me describe two of the latter kind. The first describes a conversation with Sigala, a lay person. Sigala has left home in the early morning, with his hair still wet after his bath, to pay devotion to the several quarters of the earth and sky. The Buddha meets him and asks him why he is doing this. The only answer he can give is that his father before him did so. The Buddha's response is that the best way to honour the several quarters is to create right relationships in society. After giving some general moral advice, he lists six relationships: parent/child; teacher/pupil; wife/husband; friend/friend; master/servant; lay person/mendicants and Brahmins. Honouring these is better, he insists, than performing rituals that have no social meaning. And he lists the duties that should accompany each. For instance, in the husband and wife relationship, the husband should be respectful, courteous, and faithful, handing over authority to his wife and giving her adornments. In turn, the wife should perform her duties well, offer hospitality to both families, be faithful, and watch over her husband's possessions. The point of the discourse is that the creation of harmony in society through the honouring of duties, even by those who are in positions of authority, is more important than ritual.[14]

The second discourse involves a carpenter who is dissatisfied when a wanderer, a spiritual seeker, claims that the highest skill is to do no evil, to speak no evil, to intend no evil. He goes to the Buddha for clarification. The Buddha replied humorously, 'This being so, carpenter, then ... a young baby boy lying on its back would be of abounding skill, of the highest skill, an unconquerable recluse attained to the utmost attainment.' A young baby can do no evil with his body except for a little kicking about, no evil in speech except for a little crying and no evil in intention, since a baby does not think about its own intentions. In place of this teaching, the Buddha suggests a much more activist programme of mental training to perfect intention, speech, action and livelihood.

The importance of compassion

All of this counters the stereotype that the Buddhist path is simply about gaining personal peace through withdrawal, meditation or chanting. If these discourses are taken seriously, it is also about speaking out when necessary, creating right relationships, self-sacrificial giving and compassion. At a conference of the World Conference on Religion and Peace, I once challenged a westerner who claimed that Buddhism was all about wisdom and had nothing to do with compassion. When I later shared this conversation with a prominent monk in Sri Lanka, the Venerable Piyadassi Nayake Thera, he simply said, 'Compassion is the core of Buddhism – take away compassion and there would be no Buddhism.'[15] Thomas Merton, an American Trappist monk who pioneered inter-monastic dialogue in the twentieth century, wrote of the Gal Vihāra in Polonnaruwa, which had so moved my French friend and I in 1987: 'The rock, all matter, is charged with *dharmakāya* ... everything is emptiness and everything is compassion.'[16] In using the word, *dharmakāya*, Merton was drawing on Mahāyāna Buddhism, where buddhahood has a cosmic body, a universal form that is primordially existent. The Buddha image struck him as not only representing a form of non-attachment but also universal compassion.

A famous Buddhist commentator, Buddhaghosa, who probably lived in the fifth century CE described the concept of compassion in Buddhism in this way, according to his translator, Venerable Ñānamoli:

When there is suffering in others it causes good people's hearts to be moved, thus it is compassion. Or, alternatively, it combats others' suffering and demolishes it, thus it is compassion. Or alternatively, it is scattered upon those who suffer, or extended to them by pervasion, thus it is compassion.[17]

71

First, Buddhaghosa stresses, compassion is an attitude to be developed in meditation and radiated outwards. Second, it is liberative action within society to destroy the suffering of others, to cut through it, undertaken by those who have become enlightened or who are sincerely following the path towards it. Both are rooted in the capacity of suffering to move our hearts, to touch us, although Buddhaghosa is adamant that it does not involve 'bearing others' suffering'; we are not to be weighed down by the suffering of others.[18] Rather, we are to do all we can to allay it.

It is compassion rather than love that lies at the heart of the Buddhist path and the Buddhist vision of the cosmos. The Christian concept of *agape* resonates with it rather than the generic word, 'love'. A conversation with an English-speaking Buddhist friend early into my stay in Sri Lanka helped me see why some Buddhists have a problem with the word 'love'. 'Love isn't a word that should be used in connection with the *dhamma*', my friend insisted, 'It speaks of lust or attachment. It implies choosing certain people above others and being partial. It can involve violence and the wish to possess. Some of us have stopped using the words "with love" at the end of letters. We say "with *mettā*",' she continued. I was surprised at her reaction. For a Christian, the word 'love' is usually seen as inherently positive! But I couldn't argue with it. She forced me to see how ambiguous a word 'love' is, in English. It can certainly involve attachment, even jealousy, when people say, 'I love ice cream', 'I love New York', 'I love your new dress'. In one-to-one relationships, it can also be possessive and manipulative, if one partner, through 'love' seeks to curb the freedom of the other. The Greek language needed at least three words for the concept – *agape*, *philia*, *eros*. For that Buddhist woman, compassion was preferable, because it was not linked to possessiveness or craving.

Non-attachment and compassion

So important was the relationship between withdrawal and compassionate engagement in Buddhism for me that I explored it further in an extended piece of writing completed for my Diploma in Buddhist Studies in my very first year of research.[19] Using the terms detachment and compassion, I began with questions such as: 'If compassion leads to relieving suffering and detachment to remaining aloof from the world, how can the two be practised together?' I noted that some writers on Buddhism seemed to concentrate only on detachment from the world. Edward Conze, for instance, a prominent western scholar of Buddhism, wrote that, 'The Yogin can only come into contact with the unconditioned when he brushes aside anything which is conditioned.' My conclusion, though, was that the two, detachment and compassion, were interdependent in Buddhism. Each was necessary if the other was to be truly itself. Compassion could not be true compassion if it was not undergirded by the wisdom that grew from the qualities that Buddhism links with detachment. I am still convinced that this is so and that it is something Buddhism can help Christians rediscover.

Part of the problem that I had had with the issue, I realized, came from how the Pāli was translated into English. The Pāli words usually translated as 'detachment' are *viveka* and *virāga*. The primary meaning of the first is physical withdrawal from human society. In the time of the Buddha, it was not unusual for a person to leave the household life and become an itinerant spiritual searcher or teacher, which is one form of *viveka*. The men and later women who followed the Buddha to form communities of celibate monks and nuns practised a form of *viveka* and were encouraged by the Buddha to withdraw, even from these communities, into solitude for meditation.

Viveka, as an act of physical withdrawal, I discovered, was never an end in itself in early Buddhism, although important. It was a means. If it did not lead to the cultivation of moral virtues and an effort to gain insight, the Buddha condemned it as worthless and as a practice that could lead to pride and hypocrisy. He similarly condemned the extreme asceticism that was practised by some religious groups and indeed by Siddhartha Gotama himself, until he realized that it would never lead to the enlightenment he sought. So when the Buddha is recorded in conversation with ascetics in the texts, he stresses that asceticism without the cultivation of such activist qualities as *mettā, karuṇā, muditā* and *upekkhā* is worthless.[20]

As for *virāga*, the literal meaning is without lust or without craving: *vi* (without) *rāga* (lust). A better translation than 'detachment', I decided, was 'non-attachment', non-attachment to the usual objects of *rāga*. So I wrote in my paper that, if *virāga* means without lust, it implies non-attachment to or an avoidance of things such as, 'possessiveness in relationships, defensiveness, jealousy, covetousness, acquisitiveness and competitiveness'. I added, rather triumphantly, 'There is nothing yet in this description which points to a lack of concern for humanity and the world.' Rather, I argued, it pointed to a quality that would help society to be more tolerant, harmonious and caring. If there was less *rāga*, less egotistical craving, then society would be the better for it. I also stressed that the path of *virāga* involved a struggle to discern where *rāga* was influencing one's reactions. I therefore explained that, for Buddhists, the developing of non-attachment or detachment (*virāga*) represented a movement towards seeing the true nature of things more clearly. In contrast, *sarāga* (attachment) led to biased and false perceptions, since objects would be sensed through a net of predispositions towards attraction and aversion.'[21] I compared it both to the Christian mystical tradition, where detachment from material concerns has been considered essential if there is to be a movement towards God, and to modern scientific research, where it is known that a scientist searching for one particular result (that is with an attachment to a particular result) is more likely to manipulate his data.

In summary, my argument in *Detachment and Compassion in Early Buddhism* was that *virāga* is needed within society, if it is to be healthy, and also for the practising of true compassion. I quoted a canonical discourse, the *Mahādukkhakhanda Sutta*, which makes a direct connection between attachment to sense pleasures (*rāga*) and the movement towards chaos in society. I wrote that, in the discourse,

> Greed for the possessions of another leads to disputes and contentions at the level of both the family and the nation, until 'having taken sword and shield, having girded bow and quiver, both sides mass for battle and arrows are hurled and swords are flashing'.[22]

As I will argue in the next chapter, in order for *virāga* to be developed fully, meditation is needed and that involves aloneness and withdrawal. But in itself *virāga* does not mean withdrawal. It has more to do with the forgetting of self and its concerns. And the forgetting of self, in Buddhism, is linked to the development of an active compassion.

Compassion is also embedded in Buddhist iconography. At Aukana, a lonely place in the north of Sri Lanka, there is a massive image of the Buddha that towers over the countryside. Hewn from rock, it is the largest in Sri Lanka. A standing human being barely reaches the ankles. When I travelled there, it was the sheer strength and size of the hands of the image, compared to the rest of the body, that struck me. These were hands for the saving of others, hands that could protect and guide, the hands of one who embodied compassion, who had become compassion.

A similar but unexpected experience came to me when I visited Japan. I was a member of an inter faith group from Britain that travelled at the invitation of a Japanese lay Buddhist movement,

Rissho Kosei Kai. After the other members had returned, I stayed on for a few days. One of the places I visited was Sanjūsangen-dō (The Hall of the Thirty-Three Bays), in Kyoto. It is a long, low hall dedicated to the Buddhist bodhisattva, Kannon[23] and dates back to 1164. In the centre is a seated image of Kannon and then ranged around this are 1,000 standing images, made of wood, covered with gold leaf. Each has 20 pairs of arms, which symbolize 1,000, since each arm is believed to save 25 worlds.

As I entered the hall, not really knowing what to expect, the rows of images stretched as far as my eyes could see, the palms of the main pair of hands held together, the heads framed by a halo-like structure. I wrote at the time, for a Rissho Kosei Kai journal, 'It seemed to me as though the mind which had devised the hall had asked, "How can the depth, breadth, and height of the compassion at the heart of the many worlds within our universe be conveyed?"' I continued:

The effect this had on me is hard to describe. I was filled with peace and gratitude. For some visitors, the hall was simply a museum. For me, it was a profound statement of faith. The serene grace of each statue bore silent witness to it . . . My own religious roots lie in the Methodist tradition within Protestant Christianity, which was deeply influenced by the hymns of Charles Wesley, brother of John, the Church of England clergyman who cut himself off from the established church to found Methodism in the eighteenth century. In referring to the depth, breadth and height of compassion, I intuitively echoed him.[24]

In Sanjūsangen-dō, it was the hymns of Charles Wesley that bubbled up in my body, the hymns that speak of grace at the heart of the universe, flowing through everything that exists. Buddhism and Christianity are different but for me, in that hall, they touched one another, at a profound level, in their visions of compassion – Christians might use the words grace or love – at the centre of the cosmos.

Linked with this vision of compassion is the Bodhisattva Vow, the vow of a Buddha-to-be, which I've already touched on when mentioning the arising of celestial *bodhisattvas* in the Mahāyāna tradition. Ordinary Mahāyāna Buddhists, in the mundane world, also take it, particularly monks and nuns. It commits them to remaining within the realms of birth and rebirth until all living beings in the cosmos have been liberated. In other words, even if they reach the liberation that is *nirvāṇa*, they will not stop being reborn but will return for the good of all living beings, until greed, hatred and delusion are completely eradicated.

In the middle of the twentieth century, a group of Asian Buddhists formed the International Network of Engaged Buddhists, believing that the message that activist compassion lay at the heart of the Buddhist path had somehow become lost in Buddhism. One of the founders was Thai lay Buddhist, Sulak Sivaraksa, who told me once that it was his experience of Buddhism in the West, when a student, that pushed him towards founding the Network. In the West, he found that most Buddhists considered Buddhism to be about personal transformation only. 'I felt that was escapism,' he said, 'not Buddhism or at least not the whole of Buddhism.'[25] For Sivaraksa, the Buddhist path is about making governments uncomfortable if they are causing suffering for the people and struggling against the world's cult of consumerism. His message has consistently been this:

To speak of Buddhism as something concerned with the private salvation of the individual is to ignore entirely the basic Buddhist repudiation of the notion of the individual soul. The teaching of the Buddha is not concerned with the private destiny of the individual, but with something much wider: the whole realm of sentient being, the whole consciousness. This inevitably entails a concern with social and political matters

... to attempt to understand Buddhism apart from its social dimension is mistaken. Preoccupation with the individual places limits on love, and Buddhism is an attempt to deal with what it sees as the disease of individualism.[26]

Engaged Buddhism is Buddhism that takes activist compassionate action into the heart of politics, conflict mediation and social activism.

In summary, the Buddhist path begins and ends with the eradication of greed, hatred and delusion. The path towards its eradication has the development of non-attachment and compassion at its heart, non-attachment to self and its desires, and compassion for all sentient beings. Although some contemporary Buddhists place more emphasis on withdrawal from the world than active involvement with it, the strand within Buddhist text and tradition that stresses compassionate and self-sacrificial engagement with society is strong and undergirded with textual material. But it is an engagement that is inseparable from work to eliminate personal greeds and hatreds, to develop non-attachment. Most importantly, it is a path that believes change can happen, at a personal and societal level. The fullest opportunity for change, however, is when *dāna*, *sīla* and the compassionate action that goes with it is combined with *bhāvanā* or what the West might call meditation, the subject of the next chapter.

Notes

1 *Cūḷamālunkya Sutta* (The Shorter Discourse to Mālunkyāputta), Majjhima Nikāya I, pp. 426–32, Bhikkhu Ñānamoli and Bhikkhu Bodhi (trans.), *The Middle Length Discourses of the Buddha*, Boston: Wisdom Publications, pp. 533–6.

2 See Elizabeth J. Harris, 1994, 'Detachment and Compassion' in *A Journey into Buddhism*, Kandy, Buddhist Publication Society, p. 19.

3 Sister Khema, 1986, *An Exhortation: Self-image of Self-Knowledge*,

Kandy: Buddhist Publication Society (Bodhi Leaf 105), p. 22.

4 T. W. Rhys Davids, an orientalist, translated the words as 'Work out your own salvation with diligence' but this is a Christianized version. Much better are the translations I have given, by Maurice Walsh and E. H. Brewster respectively.

5 Martin Wickramasinghe (trans. Ashley Halpe), 1985, *The Way of the Lotus: Viragaya*. Dehiwela: Tisara Prakasakayo.

6 Paul Williams with Anthony Tribe, 2000, *Buddhist Thought: A Complete Introduction to the Indian Tradition*, London and New York: Routledge, p. 102.

7 Dhammapada, vv. 129–30, K. R. Norman (trans.), 1997, *The Word of the Doctrine (Dhammapada)*, Oxford: Pāli Text Society, p. 20.

8 *Mettā Sutta* in the *Sutta Nipāta* of the *Khuddaka Nikāya* of the *Sutta Piṭaka*, v. 149, H. Saddhatissa (trans.), 1985, *Sutta Nipāta*, London: Curzon Press.

9 Adapted from Lynn de Silva, 1980, *Buddhism Beliefs and Practices in Sri Lanka*, Colombo: Ecumenical Institute for Study and Dialogue.

10 *Ambalaṭṭhikā Rāhulovada Sutta* (Discourse on an Exhortation to Rahula at Ambalaṭṭhika), *Majjhima Nikāya*, vol. II, p. 416.

11 J. F. Dickson, 1889, 'Ceylon', *The Illustrated English Magazine*, October 1889, pp. 16–25, here p. 24, quoted in Harris, 2006, *Theravāda Buddhism and the British Encounter*, p. 120.

12 The two monks were interviewed for the BBC series, *The Way of the Buddha*, and their words were quoted in Harris, 1998, *What Buddhists Believe*, pp. 112–13.

13 *Puṇṇovāda Sutta*, *Majjhima Nikāya*, vol. III, p. 269, I. B. Horner (trans.), 1990, *The Middle Length Sayings*, Oxford: Pāli Text Society, p. 321, also see Harris, 1994, *Violence and Disruption in Society*, p. 41.

14 *Sigālovāda Sutta*, *Dīgha Nikāya*, vol. III, pp. 180–90.

15 For information about the Venerable Piyadassi see, Kirthie Abeyesekera, 1995, *Piyadassi: The Wandering Monk, His Life and Times*, Colombo: Karunaratne and Sons.

16 Quoted in Elizabeth J. Harris, 1994, *A Journey into Buddhism*, Kandy: Buddhist Publication Society (Bodhi Leaves No. 134), p. 22.

17 *The Path of Purification (Visuddhimagga)*, Bhadantācariya Buddhaghosa, Bhikkhu Ñānamoli (trans.), 1991, Kandy: Buddhist

Publication Society: 310 (Section IX.91).

18 *The Path of Purification*, 310.

19 It was eventually published as: Elizabeth J. Harris, 1997, *Detachment and Compassion in Early Buddhism*, Kandy: Buddhist Publication Society (Bodhi Leaf No. 141).

20 See for example, *Udumbarikā Sīhanāda Sutta, Dīgha Nikāka*, vol. III, pp. 36ff.

21 Harris, 1997, *Detachment and Compassion*, p. 8.

22 Harris, 1997, *Detachment and Compassion*, p. 13 quoting from the *Mahādukkhakhanda Sutta* (Greater Discourse on the Stems of Anguish) *Majjhima Nikāya*, vol. I, 86–7 (I. B. Horner (trans.), 1987, *The Middle Length* Sayings, vol. I, Oxford: Pāli Text Society, pp. 113–14.

23 Kannon is the Japanese form of Avalokiteśvara, an important bodhisattva in Mahāyāna Buddhism because of his compassion. He is the main patron bodhisattva of Tibet.

24 Elizabeth J. Harris, 1998, 'World Religions are not the same, nor are they different' in *Dharma World*, vol. 25, pp. 7–20, here p. 7.

25 Quoted in Harris, 1998, *What Buddhists Believe*, p. 100.

26 S. Sivaraksa, 1994, *A Buddhist Vision for Renewing Society: Collected Articles by a Concerned Thai Intellectual*, Bangkok: The Inter-Religious Commission for Development, p. 162.

4

Mind and Meditation

In Autumn 1992, I recorded several four-minute talks for the 'Words of Faith' slot in the BBC World Service schedule of religious programmes. One of them was on meditation and it included these words:

> Once I told an academic in Sri Lanka that I practised a Buddhist form of meditation. Flippantly, he asked whether I was able to levitate. That's not an uncommon reaction. It confuses meditation with self-induced trance or making the mind a blank, something that is unrelated to everyday life. But to make such a confusion is a mistake. True Buddhist meditation is a vigorous form of mind-training which can transform both thought and action . . .
>
> One monk who taught me put it this way: 'Meditation is the ultimate practice of non-violence. Suffering, pain and feelings of anger are not suppressed but faced, confronted and transformed'.[1]

At the time of the broadcast, I had been practising Buddhist meditation for six years under different teachers. However, the words I quoted in the last seconds were actually said by the monk who led my first meditation session in Sri Lanka – the time I walked with trepidation into a lay Buddhist woman's home, forgetting at first to take off my shoes. They drew me in and made me eager to know more. And the more I have learnt, the more I see the truth of his words. If I had given those 'Words of Faith' now, though, I would have stressed that it is more than the mind that is transformed. It is the whole person.

For Buddhists, meditation complements ethical living and the pro-active development of loving kindness and compassion, by calming and shaping the body, mind and heart. It helps Buddhists to 'see' and uproot their greed, hatred and delusion. One of the programmes in my radio series, *The Way of the Buddha*, was, naturally, on meditation. Among the Buddhist voices it included were those of Helen Jandamit (a lay Buddhist meditation teacher living in Bangkok), Niramon Prudtatorn (an activist for women's rights, at Wongsanit Ashram, the home of an Engaged Buddhist Community just outside Bangkok), Professor Jotiya Dhirasekara (one of my first academic teachers in Sri Lanka, now the Venerable Dhammavihari) and the sole Christian I interviewed for the programmes, Aloysius Pieris. Helen began by quoting verse 183 from the Dhammapada:

The teaching of the Buddha is, 'do good, avoid evil and purify the mind'.[2] Meditation is about purifying the mind. It is very difficult to avoid evil if your mind is not pure because you're dragged in there whether you want to be or not. And it is the same for doing good. Sometimes we're doing good for all the wrong reasons but if you purify your mind then you're able to see clearly what you are doing and determine how much or how little to do and what is right and what is wrong.

Niramon immediately placed meditation in the context of her activism:

To have the opportunity to do meditation, to look inside myself, to learn how to cope with greed, anger, hatred and ignorance, this has been very helpful in my life, for my spiritual development. If women have more spiritual sanctuary,

women can gain self-esteem. As activists, we can help them
to be more peaceful, not to be just angry, protesting all the
time. If we can help women activists to practise meditation,
it would help them to be broader in their ideas, so that they
can go further than merely rallying on the street. If we practise
more, we will gain more compassion and more calm to deal
with the many issues, not just prostitution, but also rape cases
and many other injustices in society.

The Venerable Dhammavihari drew on the same idea of cleansing that Helen had used:

Bhāvanā should not be the mere ability to fix your mind on
the bulb that is burning on the ceiling or the glow of a light
on the wall but it is to know that you have gradually peeled off
the stains of contamination in your mind – conflict, ill-will,
jealousy, rivalry. It is a question of how clean your inside is.

It is significant that he used the Pāli term, *bhāvanā*, not 'meditation', the third in the triad I mentioned in the last chapter.
Meditation is a western term that is not a direct translation of
the words used in Sanskrit and Pāli. The term *bhāvanā* is from
a causative verb, 'to bring into being'. *Bhāvanā*, meditation, is,
therefore, about development, cultivation, the bringing into
being of something. And it was this that Aloysius Pieris stressed.
It was the bringing into being of the fruit of seeing and eradicating one's greed, hatred and delusion, namely, greedlessness:

The ultimate goal of meditation is greedlessness, *taṇhā nirodha*
(the ceasing of craving), which is really a definition of *nibbāna*.
The purpose of meditation is that. It's not just an ego trip to
another world. It is simply a hard, committed, continuous,
uninterrupted effort at eradicating the egocentric building of
a world around yourself. It is to break those barriers and to

be free enough not only to enjoy the freedom yourself but to share it with others.[3]

Samatha and *vipassanā*

In this chapter I will build on these voices from Asia in order to share what the Buddhist meditation practices that I have been taught can offer. What I have been taught forms just one part of a wealth of meditation practices within Buddhism's different schools. So this chapter will only touch the surface. Nevertheless, there is a unity across schools, because most practices fall into two basic types: *samatha* and *vipassanā*. My experience is that they are not completely distinct. They both touch each other and diverge. But I will describe them separately.

The word, *samatha*, literally means tranquillity or calm. *Samatha* meditation brings the meditator towards a state of tranquillity, relaxation and one-pointedness, emotionally, mentally and in the body, through concentration on an object. According to Buddhist tradition, *samatha* meditation alone cannot lead to liberation but it can lead to the calmness, clarity and flexibility of mind that creates the conditions for wisdom and liberation.[4] The breath, either as it comes in and out of the nostrils or as it causes the abdomen to rise, is the most frequently used object.

A certain posture is recommended for both types of meditation. The yogic lotus position is ideal. Sitting cross-legged with a cushion is also good. If this is not possible – and it was never possible for me – then the body should be held so that the back is completely straight. Now, I tend to use a prayer stool. Perhaps it is worth adding, though, that there are no hard and fast rules about this. Western meditation teacher, Sarah Shaw, points to the fact that the companion of the Buddha, Ananda, after much determined meditation practice, is said to have gained enlightenment when getting into bed.[5]

The Pāli texts describe the beginnings of meditation for a monk or *bhikkhu* in these words:

He ... finds a solitary lodging, at the foot of a forest tree, in a mountain cave or gorge, a charnel-ground, a jungle-thicket, or in the open air on a heap of straw. Then, having eaten after his return from the alms-round, he sits down cross-legged, holding his body erect, and concentrates on keeping mindfulness established before him.

Abandoning worldly desires, he dwells with a mind freed from worldly desires, and his mind is purified of them. Abandoning ill-will and hatred ... and by compassionate love for the welfare of all beings, his mind is purified of ill-will and hatred. Abandoning sloth and torpor ... perceiving light, mindful and clearly aware, his mind is purified of sloth and torpor. Abandoning worry and flurry ... and with an inwardly calmed mind his heart is purified of worry and flurry. Abandoning doubt, he dwells with doubt left behind, without uncertainty as to what things are wholesome, his mind is purified of doubt.[6]

Mindfulness is a key concept in Buddhist meditation, which I will return to. As for worldly desires, ill-will and hatred, sloth and torpor, worry and flurry, and doubt, these are the five hindrances to meditation mentioned in the texts. A meditator will do all he or she can to overcome them.

When the attention is focused on the breath in *samatha* meditation, thoughts and feelings come into the mind unbidden, without our willing them. When this happens the mind is gently, not forcibly, brought back to the breath. If this happens consistently then we should do this, according to Mithra Wettimuny, a Sri Lankan lay meditation teacher:

When the mind strays to another object, what you must do is to bring forth mindfulness again. Be mindful that it has strayed. Don't try to force it back to the breath, because when you force you get tired and fatigue is not good for this practice. Patiently wait, being mindful and aware that your mind has strayed. When you are mindful and aware, it will naturally come back to your main object, which is the breathing. Even here, it is right mindfulness that is used.[7]

According to all the meditation teachers I have had, being aware of the arising and passing of thoughts in the mind teaches impermanence and non-self. For as we sit and notice thoughts entering and passing, we realize that they are beyond our control. We cannot force our minds to be still by commanding thoughts to leave. Without our willing, they seem to be programmed to replay conversations or to plan the future. Therefore, Buddhist meditation teachers point out, how can they be 'ours'? All we can do is notice our thoughts and try to draw our attention back to our breath. It is at points such as these that *samatha* meditation touches *vipassanā*, the gaining of insight.

One of the fruits of *samatha* meditation is what Pāli Buddhism calls the *jhānas* and the Sanskrit tradition, the *dhyana*. 'Meditative absorption' is one common translation. But again there is no exact equivalent in English. They are not exactly trances, but they are heightened states of consciousness. There are two sets of four. The first set moves from a state of joy and happiness to one of complete equanimity. The first *jhāna* in the first set is described in the texts in this way:

And when he knows that these five hindrances have left him, gladness arises in him, from gladness comes delight, from the delight in his mind, his body is tranquilised, with a tranquil body he feels joy, and with joy his mind is concentrated. Being thus detached from sense-desires, detached from unwholesome states, he enters and remains in the first jhāna, which is with thinking and pondering, born of detachment, filled with delight and joy. And with this delight and joy born of detachment, he so suffuses, drenches, fills and irradiates his body that there is no spot in his entire body that is untouched by this delight and joy born of detachment.[8]

The description of the second is similar. It is 'without thinking and pondering, born of concentration, filled with delight and joy'. In the third and fourth, mindfulness and equanimity take the place of delight and joy. The fourth is described as 'beyond pleasure and pain'. The body is suffused with, 'mental purity and clarification'.[9] The simile used is that of a person wrapped from head to foot in a white garment. The second four are called 'formless' and are linked with the higher powers of the mind. In the *jhānas* the sense of self is gradually annihilated and with it any urges towards greed and hatred. Calmness, equanimity and heightened consciousness take their place.

It takes many hours of practice to reach the *jhānas*. I have certainly glimpsed the first and perhaps the second but the complete equanimity and purity that are characteristic of the last two are more difficult. *Samatha* meditation is not unique to Buddhism. The description of the *jhānas* that I have just given has links with mystical prayer in the Christian tradition.

Bare attention and seeing clearly

The literal meaning of *vipassanā* is to 'see clearly'. It aims at insight into reality and wisdom. In my first months in Sri Lanka, this caused me a problem. My teachers were telling me that this insight would be into *anicca*, *dukkha* and *anattā*, and, as I said in Chapter 1, I wondered whether I wanted to see these characteristics as truth. I eventually decided to allow the methods I had used in Christian contemplation to move into the background to allow me to use Buddhist methods and to see what happened. In retrospect I know the decision was right. I came to see that *vipassanā* meditation can offer a radical window on the mind, the heart and even the subconscious. It is a form of mind culture that I have come to believe is essential for self-knowledge and for effective action in the world, not only for Buddhists but anyone. It is significant that the form of meditation to which at first I was most resistant became the form that has given me the most enrichment. Yes, I saw into the reality that is *anicca*, impermanence, and gained a greater awareness of *dukkha* but, more important than this, I gained insight into my own greeds and hatreds. For me, as a Christian, the method became complementary to prayer. As for *anattā*, let me leave that to a later chapter. Before I share what *vipassanā* meditation has meant to me, let me first say more about Nilambe.

Nilambe was a wonderful place to explore what these two forms of meditation involved. Some meditation teachers in Sri Lanka looked down on it, believing it to be far too lax and rather syncretistic. Westerner meditators, for instance, could practise yoga, a Hindu practice, in the morning if they wanted to. Yet, I would want to defend Nilambe and Godwin Samararatne (1932–2000), who was then the lay Buddhist Director of the Centre. Godwin was a remarkable meditation teacher, who, before his premature death, became known in Europe and South Africa. Jeanne Mynett's description of him on Godwin's homepage, set up after his death by some of his pupils, is most fitting:

What was so special about Godwin was that he lived what he taught – his teaching and his life were seamless. He had the marvellous ability to put the teachings of the Buddha concerning suffering and the way out of suffering into his own simple words which were relevant to the everyday lives and experience of the people he was speaking to, both Buddhist and non-Buddhist.

Godwin's deepest concern was to help people free themselves from their suffering, and having realised the fruits of the

Buddha's teaching himself, he brought a great depth of wisdom and compassion to his explorations of the Dhamma with others. He also evinced a lightness, humour, and sense of the absurd, as much in his talks as in his day-to-day life.[10]

Whenever I went to Nilambe, there was a diverse bunch of people meditating – Sri Lankan and western, Buddhist and non-Buddhist. As I have already said, the daily schedule was strict, although not as strict as at some other Sri Lankan meditation centres, where the day can begin at 3.00 or 4.00 a.m. Here, the first meditation session began at 5.00 and lasted until 6.00. Yoga followed for those who wanted it. Breakfast – rice porridge, soya grits and perhaps fruit – was at 7.30. This was followed by work – cleaning the toilets, weeding the gardens, sweeping the rooms. Between 9.30 and 11.00 there was another period of meditation, which included sitting and walking meditation.[11] Between 11.00 and 12.00 we were free to follow our own practice. The main meal of the day was at noon. It was always vegetarian, usually red rice, lentils and vegetables. After this there was a period for rest, walking or reading, during which we could arrange individual sessions of guidance with Godwin. Between 15.00 and 16.00, there was another session of meditation in the hall, followed by tea. We could then do our own practice and watch the sun set. There was a further hour of meditation between 18.30 and 19.30, followed by another drink (and a snack for those who could not manage to fast until breakfast) and then a discussion period. We were usually lighting our candles in our *kutees*, or cells, by 21.30. There was, after all, no electricity at Nilambe.

Notices were placed around the Centre reminding people of the attitudes to be cultivated. Near the women's *kutees* was something like this, 'Do not kill any living thing. Do not take that which is not given. Have little contact between the sexes. Keep Noble Silence. Do not take intoxicating liquor or drugs. Wear light coloured clothing, no shorts, no sleeveless tops.'

My first introduction to what has become for me a basic *vipassanā* practice, that of bare attention, came on my first visit. Although I have already briefly described it, it needs to be repeated here as well. Godwin described the practice in this way, 'Allow thoughts to rise freely without controlling or willing them. If no thoughts arise, fix your mind on a sound. Observe your thoughts as if they belonged to someone else. Let them arise and pass. If you judge them, be aware that that is what you are doing. Tell your body that you are willing to feel sensations. If they come, do not repress them. Do not judge them. Notice them and know them. If you feel any emotions, recognize them – pain, anger, happiness, peace . . .'[12]

It is a form of practice that involves complete openness to the present moment without having an object to which concentration is returned. Anything is allowed to enter the mind or the heart, whether this is anger, jealousy, love, aversion, memories, hopes for the future, pain or sadness, or simply irritation at a noise, the light touch of a mosquito's legs on the arm or a persistent itch on the skin of the face. Nothing that arises is judged good or bad. Even if a strong urge to murder someone arises, it is not condemned. Nothing is clung to or developed. Nothing is repressed. Thoughts and feelings are noticed and allowed to pass, both those that are triggered by the immediate surroundings and those that arise from inner depths. All are to be noticed. In this way, the meditator gradually becomes aware of how her mind reacts to what is unpleasant and pleasant, what it is drawn to and what it cowers from, what it claims as 'mine' and what it rejects, and perhaps what it has hidden from consciousness.

In a similar way to *samatha* meditation, what comes into the mind and heart (one of the Pāli words translated as mind, *citta*, actually encompasses mind and heart) in the meditation of bare attention is not owned as 'mine'. In Buddhism, what arises and passes cannot be permanent possessions. They cannot be 'me'. If this is accepted, it becomes easier to recognize rather than repress what arises, not clinging to it, on the one hand, or pushing it aside with hatred or disgust, on the other. This kind of attitude can be illustrated by the advice Buddhist meditation teachers give when there is a persistent pain or itch in the body. Our usual reaction is to scratch the itch or move a limb. 'No!' a meditation teacher will say. 'Do not move. Make the pain the object of your meditation. See it simply as pain rather than as "my" pain. And it will pass.' From my first experience of this teaching in my first Buddhist meditation session, my experience is that the discomfort does pass, quite quickly, and with it the urge to scratch or move.

The practice draws on a concept that I have already mentioned several times, known in Pāli as *sati* and translated as mindfulness. It is central to both types of meditation. In *samatha* the medita-tor is 'mindful' of one object in order to gain one-pointedness of mind. And it is mindfulness that brings the mind back to the object, to the present, when it strays. In *vipassanā* meditation mindfulness is linked with the continual effort to remain in the present, watching what arises in the mind and body. One impor-tant discourse in the Pāli texts that speaks of this outlines four foundations for mindfulness: mindfulness of the body; mind-fulness of the feelings; mindfulness of the mind (for instance, knowing whether the mind is affected by greed, hatred or delu-sion); and mindfulness of 'mind-objects' such as whether the five hindrances are present or how the senses are responding to sen-sory stimulation. The opening paragraph of the discourse states, using the translation of a western monk, Bhikkhu Bodhi, 'This is the direct path for the purification of beings, for the surmount-ing of sorrow and lamentation, for the disappearance of pain and grief, for the attainment of the true way, for the realisation of Nibbāna.'[13] Bhikkhu Bodhi contrasts this with the way of the *jhānas*, which can, in its higher stages, lead the meditator away from the path to *nibbāna*.

I can remember going into some meditation sessions with a pleasant feeling of anticipation of what would come if I allowed my body, mind and heart complete freedom to throw up what it wanted, in the practice of bare attention. In some sessions, nothing much arose and I would find myself either watching my breath or being taken over by agitation or sleepiness. In others, things were more dramatic. In one session, an incredible amount of anger emerged from repressed depths so that I found myself saying inwardly words I would never say in public, 'Why the bloody hell am I sitting here? This is useless. There's no bloody reason why I should be subjecting myself to such torture. I can't bear it. What on earth do I think I'm doing?'[14] Before this, I had thought myself a calm person! It was the first time I had really looked my anger in the face – but not the last.

Godwin's teaching was that everything that arose in our minds or bodies could be our teacher. Confused states of mind could be our teachers. Thoughts or feelings that society would condemn could be our teachers. So often, he explained in one teaching session, we have an image of ourselves that has been created by the expectations we think others have of us. When emotions arise that do not fit in with this image, we hate them and ourselves. If anger appears in meditation, we hate it, thus doubling its destructive power. And the same for jealousy or hatred. 'Meditation should be an opportunity to make our demons our friends', he would explain. When meditation was causing confusion and some mental pain, when what was arising in meditation ran counter to our stereotype of meditation, we should not be discouraged. The fruits could be positive. For we were beginning to face our darker sides, and only through doing this could we move forward. If we were to make our demons our friends, however, it was necessary to face whatever arose in a non-attached way and to allow repressed emotions space. Meditation was not about self-torture but about freedom and letting go into the present moment. The anger that arose in my own meditation practice was just one of my own demons that meditation uncovered.

In Godwin's teaching, there was a therapy that helped many

westerners who came to Nilambe, some of whom were emotionally damaged. Godwin helped them to face their problems, through encouraging them to watch whatever arose in their minds and hearts silently, non-judgementally and with loving kindness towards themselves. Always there was an emphasis on friendliness towards self. We were never advised to radiate loving kindness to others without first surrounding ourselves with it.

Godwin also gave people a programme for mindfulness outside the meditation hall at Nilambe that went something like this. First, slow down all movements. Go to the point of exaggerating movements in order to be aware of them. Then, begin to watch your intentions. See if you can catch your mind as it makes the intention to sit, wash a dish or walk. After this, work with your thoughts. Watch them. Do they come because you want them? Watch them form and pass. At certain points in the day, relive your thought and actions. Were there successes or failures? If so, note them without censure. Work with your emotions, both positive and negative. If you feel joy or serenity, recognize this. If you feel restlessness, anxiety, doubt or sluggishness, recognize this. Recognize your emotions without being attached to them. Just be with them, accept them. Adopt a neutral attitude to them. Develop a 'mirror mind' that simply sees what is there without clouding the image with joy or censure. Keep noble silence. Observe the intention or the need to speak. Observe the boredom this might bring. Be aware of sounds and seeing. Try to hear and see without past associations and labelling. Try not to label a sound or label a person. See without naming. See colour and form rather than a label.[15]

I believe the teaching I received at Nilambe from Godwin was consistent with the very heart of Buddhism. Buddhism's message is basically that our dis-ease is due to what is buried in our minds and hearts, because of the way we have conditioned our minds to react since birth, or, some Buddhists would say, over numerous births. The task of the mindfulness that is *vipassanā* is to de-clutter, to bring to light, to detoxify. A book that has had a profound effect on me and on many others is *The Power of Mindfulness* by a German convert to Buddhism, the Venerable Nyanaponika (born Siegmund Feniger, 1901–94), who spent most of his life as a Buddhist monk in Sri Lanka. Godwin's use of the term, 'bare attention' probably came from him. Both used it to explain the use of mindfulness in *vipassanā* meditation, inspired by the *Satipaṭṭhāna Sutta*. Nyanaponika spoke of the benefits in this way:

> It is the dark, untidy corners of the mind where our most dangerous enemies dwell. From there, they attack us unawares, and much too often they succeed in defeating us. That twilight world peopled by frustrated desires and suppressed resentments, by vacillations and whims and many other shadowy figures, forms a background from which upsurging passions – greed, lust, hatred and anger – may derive powerful support ... But how to deal with that unwieldy, tangled mass? ... the only safe remedy is just to face it – with mindfulness. Nothing more difficult is needed than to acquire the habit of noticing these rudimentary thoughts as often as possible by directing bare attention to them.[16]

Important to stress is that this practice not only concerns thoughts but feelings and sense awareness as well. Buddhism would say that there are three basic types of feelings: feelings of attraction, feelings of aversion and feelings that are neutral. Throughout our lives our sense awareness is conditioned to develop into one of these in response to different triggers. Spiders, snakes, body fluids or obesity may trigger aversion, a shrinking away. Sunlight, warmth, vibrant colour, clear air, physical beauty or a fat bank balance may trigger attraction and expansive openness. There are also the reactions that are linked to the promotion of our self-image, the promotion of the 'I' and the 'mine', where our default setting usually concerns whether an action is in harmony or disharmony with our self-image. Watching, in meditation, how our mind reacts can help us detect and transform this default setting. And it spills out from the meditation room into everyday life.

Let me give an example that I used in the 'Words of Faith' with which I began this chapter. Thinking of a period spent at Nilambe, I said:

At one meditation centre in Sri Lanka, high in the mountains, surrounded by tea estates, the first session begins at five in the morning. I had to get up by candlelight, pull on warm clothes, and cross the grass to the meditation hall, under a sky often brilliantly full of stars. One morning, I was gazing at the dark, silvered beauty of the sky when I heard steps below me. At that moment, I caught my mind saying, 'Go on into the meditation hall so that they can see you were up first'. Normally, I would have hurried into the hall to show punctuality, but on that occasion I noted the thought, recognised the element of competition, and consciously refused to act on it. I stayed for several more moments wrapt in the pre-dawn stillness, feeling the cool air against my skin, and I was certainly not the first to settle my cushions before the silent candle-lit image of the Buddha. And I know it was the practice of *sati*, of mindfulness, which made that moment of insight into my own competitive egotism possible, insight into a childish wish to impress, to be top of the class.[17]

The texts might have called that a case of 'guarding the doors of the senses', which is an important part of the reflective Buddhist path. The training that is meditation should result in us being able to catch the moments between sense contact or awareness, and the arising of feelings of attraction and aversion.

There have been other such moments since then. What is important is that the practice of mindfulness or bare attention gives us insight into how our attractions and aversions are linked to our self-image and our self-promotion. It gives us insight into what triggers competitiveness, defensiveness, jealousy or feelings of inadequacy. Buddhism would say that none of these urges is 'ours' and that we need to cut through them. I started to do this when I recognized competitiveness coming into my own mind on that faraway morning in Sri Lanka. And the journey continues.

Purifying the perceptions by losing 'I' and 'mine'

There are many other fruits of meditation. One is that our perception becomes purer because the 'I' becomes less. As meditation can teach us that pain is simply pain and not 'my' pain, so seeing can become simply seeing rather than 'my' seeing, overladen with all our conditioned reactions. Personally, I've still a long way to go if I am to have the 'mirror mind' that Godwin talked about, but I may have glimpsed *anattā* and *anicca* on one return train journey to Colombo from Nilambe, when I wrote this in my diary:

Mist, an early morning, white, numinous touching, blurred the hills and the paddy fields. White birds rose up from the water. An occasional blue or green flashed among the trees, in brilliant colour. Everything had a touch of enchantment. At one point, my mind was only aware of movement – the movement of ballet or dance when the dancer becomes pure movement. Suddenly, the Buddhist concept of the body and the world as a series of processes became clearer. The idea of static entities suddenly seemed ridiculous. Everything was moving. My seeing seemed no longer to be an appendage of my individual body but a cosmic process working through me. 'Seeing' became a gift, an exciting and changing thing. The fields became greener and the mist more beautiful. 'Seeing' was happening through me without thought dominating it. I realized that to think of the senses as processes rather than my possession was not to diminish them but to enhance the wonder of seeing, hearing, touching. *Anicca* and *anattā* suddenly became clear, not as a doctrine but as experience.[18]

It was an experience of losing the usual commentary we have in our minds when we view the world. The 'I' of that commentary was gone and everything appeared more beautiful.

Buddhists insist that our physical pain can also be made more bearable if the 'I' and 'mine' is taken out. I have learnt much from Buddhist friends about this and have tried to bring it into my own life. For instance, an elderly friend of mine once walked up Sri Pada in Sri Lanka during the pilgrimage season between December and May. Sri Pada is a holy mountain, over 7,000 feet high. On one of the ascents, steps have been inserted into the mountain from top to bottom. Pilgrims usually climb at night so that they are on the top to see the sun rise. In the season, thousands of pilgrims ascend this illuminated staircase, which, from a distance, looks like a diamond necklace thrown down the mountain's side. When my friend climbed up, the crowd was so large that the pilgrims had to pause at every step. The pressure on the leg muscles was incredible. My friend told me that the only way she could force her legs through the ordeal was to say of the pain, 'This pain is not mine, this is not me. It is simply pain.' Long years of meditation practice had made this possible.[19] Such practice also makes us keenly aware of the pain of others.

Meditation for the social activist

Niramon Prudtatorn, at the beginning of this chapter, stressed that meditation was necessary for the social activist. In Buddhism there should be no separation between meditation and action. Niramon, when I interviewed her, was part of a socially engaged Buddhist community just outside Bangkok. Everyone I interviewed there said that meditation was central to their activism because, without meditation, their activism would be driven by anger or hatred towards the 'oppressor', emotions that lead to burn-out, ineffective action and blindness. So, one of the most important things that Buddhism has helped me to see is that meditation, or *bhāvanā* is an essential complement to the path outlined in the last chapter. So, Pracha Hutanawatr, another member of the community near Bangkok, said this:

> Meditation helped me develop a deep sense of humour. And this is very important for life, because, as an activist, you are so serious. You want to change the world. You want to change the people. You want to change the social structure. But in meditation you can see that all the oppressive forces are also within you at the same time . . . If you have no sense of humour then you burn yourself out.[20]

Action without the physical inaction of meditation can be flawed, engaged Buddhists would say. Unless we know how our own mind works, we can so easily project our failings onto others and fail to stand in their shoes.

Meditation on death and impermanence

This chapter cannot end without mention of forms of Buddhist meditation that are focused on objects other than the breath. Meditation on the impermanence of our own bodies, and by extension, our own death, is an important practice for many Buddhists. It is not unusual for there to be a skeleton or some other reminder of death in meditation halls or the individual cells of monks and nuns. The Venerable Ayya Khema, while in Sri Lanka, established a meditation centre for women on an island in a lake in the south, Parappaduwa. On one side wall of the meditation room was a life-size skeleton to aid meditation on the impermanence of our own bodies. And in the porch of Sr Nyanasiri's small *kutee* in Kandy was a picture of a shady figure coming towards the viewer – the figure of death. Both were a reminder that death can come at any time and that we need to be prepared for it, as well as for the slow decay of our bodies. Again, Buddhism has taught me that this is not morbid. It is realistic, even healthy. For if we push death away from us, we deny what it is to be embodied and live in the delusion that what we have will last for ever. When death eventually came towards my dear friend, Nyanasiri, she was, I am sure, more ready for it.

Acceptance of our impermanence is often linked to seeing impermanence in nature. Time at a meditation centre or mindfulness as part of one's life can lead to a poignant awareness of this. At Nilambe, I once wrote:

What a lesson in impermanence is the changing aspect of the hills. As dawn broke this morning, the further hills were invisible behind mist. The air was full of droplets. Wet grass stroked my bare feet. But by 9 a.m. the hills were washed with sunlight. Every peak was clear. Then, as the sun journeyed, they absorbed different moods of colour – golden, green and grey, until all colour was eliminated and only shapes were drawn in the light of the moon.[21]

Within the Theravāda Buddhist tradition, not all *bhikkhus* live in community. Some choose to be hermits, sometimes living in caves. One such hermit *bhikkhu* that I came to know was the Venerable Sumedha, a western artist who converted to Buddhism. He was born in 1932 in Switzerland and trained at the École des Beaux Arts in Geneva and Paris. In 1970, he came to Sri Lanka and, when I first spoke to him, had been living in a cave near Kandy for about 16 years. This is what he said to me in an interview:

Complete silence is like a metaphor. But I would say when the silence is such that you can hear your heart beat, your breath and an ant walking on a piece of paper, then it is quite silent. There is definitely a silence when you can hear your own thoughts ... The whole physical environment with time becomes a preacher, a teacher, a piece of art. Whatever we see turns into a thought regarding *Dhamma*. If we see roots growing over, we see craving; if we see falling leaves and decay, we see impermanence and the tenacity of impermanence, despite the fact that things grow again and again and again. Things are our teachers in so far as we are aware that we are looking, aware that we can easily fall into the trap of seeing the world in the hallucination of stability and ownership and happiness.[22]

Meditation and loving kindness

Awareness of death and impermanence is also closely linked, in Buddhism, to the outflowing of loving kindness and compassion. Compassion as well as insight is a fruit of the greedlessness that meditation should help to arise. One of the most moving meditations in Buddhism for me is the meditation on loving kindness, *mettā* the first of the four 'divine abidings'. Many Buddhists practise this every day and it goes back to the very beginnings of Buddhism to the discourse mentioned in the last chapter, which has these words at its heart:

Just as a mother would protect her only child at the risk of her own life, even so, let a person cultivate a boundless heart towards all beings.

Let his thoughts of boundless love pervade the whole world; above, below and across without any obstruction, without any hatred, without any enmity.[23]

In a traditional meditation on loving kindness, one begins with self and imagines loving kindness embracing every part of one's body and mind with the words, 'May I be happy and free from suffering'. Then one brings to mind a respected teacher and surrounds that person with loving kindness. Next, loving kindness is radiated to a dearly loved friend or family member. Then it is sent out towards a person for whom one feels nothing very much. Lastly, one imagines it surrounding a hostile person or an enemy.[24]

In contemporary meditation practice, teachers usually bring in more objects but, always, the meditation includes surrounding those who we do not like, who could be considered enemies, with loving kindness. When leading groups in this form of meditation, I have sometimes used a form that the Venerable Ayya Khema first introduced me to, at the end of a meditation day she gave to a group of women in Colombo. My adapted form of her meditation goes like this:

Let us imagine that loving kindness is radiating from our being into the whole world.

Imagine there is a white lotus flower opening inside your heart. From it, there flows a golden stream of light, the stream of loving kindness. It flows around you, flooding your body with warmth. Allow it to spread around you. Give loving kindness to yourself and to your body. May you be well. May you be happy.

Now let the stream of light and love flow from you to those near to you – in this room. They are your sisters and brothers, sharing the same journey through life as you. May they be happy. May they be well.

Now let the stream leap out of the building where you are to your family members. Let their faces come into your mind. Thank them for all they have done for you. Forgive them if they have hurt you. Spread love and care towards them. Dead or living, think of them with kindness.

Now, in your imagination, go along the streets of your neighbourhood. Throw out the stream of loving kindness to all your neighbours, young and old, friendly and unfriendly. Surround with love those you like and those you do not.

Now, extend loving kindness to those who are suffering in this country. Send loving kindness to any places where there is deprivation, poverty or tension. Be aware of the suffering and pain in these situations. Send a golden stream of light into the hardship and violence.

Reach beyond your country now. Send out the golden stream to the whole world of women, men and children – to places where there is rejoicing and to places where there is mourning, to places of war, to places where there is starvation or persecution, to places suffering from natural disasters. Feel a sense of unity with all people everywhere.

Picture also the world of animals and plants, trees and rivers, mountains and seas. Spread loving kindness, joy and compassion to the world in its entirety.

Now take the golden thread inwards again. Surround yourself with loving kindness. Allow the light to rest in your own heart ready to be used again.

Meditation is an essential part of the developing of engaged, activist compassion mentioned in the previous chapter and also, within Buddhist thought, of the path towards wisdom.

Notes

1 Elizabeth J. Harris, 1994, *A Journey into Buddhism* (Bodhi Leaf No. 134), Kandy: Buddhist Publication Society, pp. 4–6.

2 The full verse 183 of the Dhammapada, using the translation of K. R. Norman, 1997, *The Word of the Doctrine*, Oxford: Pāli Text Society, p. 28, is, 'The avoidance of all evil; the undertaking of good; the cleansing of one's mind; this is the teaching of the awakened ones.'

3 Quotations taken from interviews conducted by Elizabeth Harris for the BBC in 1995–6, published in Harris, 1998, *What Buddhists Believe*, pp. 66–8.

4 See, for instance, Sarah Shaw, 2006, *Buddhist Meditation: An Anthology of Texts from the Pāli Canon*, London and New York: Routledge, pp. 2–3.

5 Shaw, 2006, *Buddhist Meditation*, p. 18.

6 This passage appears in several discourses, for instance: *Sāmaññaphala Sutta*, *Dīgha Nikāya*, vol. I, p. 71, Maurice Walsh (trans.), 1995, *The Long Discourses of the Buddha*, Boston: Wisdom Publications, p. 101.

7 Harris, 1998, *What Buddhists Believe*, p. 70.

8 *Sāmaññaphala Sutta*, *Dīgha Nikāya*, vol. I 73, Walshe, 1995, *The Long Discourses of the Buddha*, p. 102.

9 *Sāmaññaphala Sutta*, *Dīgha Nikāya*, vol. I 75, Walshe, 1995, *The Long Discourses of the Buddha*, p. 103.

10 From: 'Introduction to Godwin Samararatne', Jeanne Mynett, 2005, on www.godwin-home-page.net.

11 Walking meditation is a form of mindfulness training. One walks slowly, noticing the intention to raise each foot and place it down on the floor, staying completely in the present moment.

12 Unpublished diary 6 September 1986.

13 *Satipaṭṭhāna Sutta*, *Majjhima Nikāya*, vol. I, pp. 55–6, Bhikkhu Ñānamoli and Bhikkhu Bodhi (trans.), 1995, *The Middle Discourses of the Buddha*, Boston: Wisdom Publications, p. 145.

14 Unpublished diary, 15 December 1986.

15 Unpublished diary, 23 October 1987.

16 Nyanaponika Thera, 1968 (1980), *The Power of Mindfulness*,

Kandy: Buddhist Publication Society, p. 8.

17 Harris, 1994, *A Journey into Buddhism*, pp. 5–6.

18 Unpublished diary, 23 December 1986, this part published in Harris, 2002, 'The Beginning of Something Being Broken', pp. 13–14.

19 See Harris, 1994, *A Journey into Buddhism*, pp. 16–19.

20 Harris, 1998, *What Buddhists Believe*, p. 66.

21 Unpublished diary, 16 December 1986.

22 Part of an interview carried out for the BBC series, *The Way of the Buddha*, extracts reprinted in Harris, 1998, *What Buddhists Believe*, p. 96.

23 Adapted from: H. Saddhatissa (trans.), 1985, *The Sutta Nipāta*, London: Curzon, p. 16 (*Sutta Nipāta* verses 149–50).

24 Based on the advice given in the sixth century CE commentary of Buddhaghosa, the *Visuddhimagga* IX 8–13, Bhikkhu Ñānamoli (trans.), 1975 (1991), *The Path of Purification by Bhadantācariya Buddhaghosa*, Kandy: Buddhist Publication Society, pp. 289–90.

5

Buddhism and Violence

I was at a conference at the Naga Vihāra in Kotte near Colombo. It was in 1988 when the Indian Peacekeeping Force was battling against the Liberation Tigers of Tamil Eelam (LTTE) in the north of the country and the Janatha Vimukti Peramuna (JVP) was rising in the south. The main speaker was a monk from Thailand. He began by assuming that everyone present was aware that the world was violent. Buddhism did not try to escape from this, he stressed. But the true victory, he continued, was to face violence with non-violence. The real enemies of humanity were the defilements of fanaticism, hatred, anger, discrimination and consumerism. To overcome anger by anger was not the Buddhist way – neither was passivity. Non-violence was the middle way between passivity and aggression and he listed three mechanisms for this. The first was to counter the negative images the parties in a conflict had towards one another. The second was to hold non-violent demonstrations. The third was to challenge the support of the population for violence. Moving to Sri Lanka, he recognized that many believed that Buddhism was threatened in the country. 'But what do you mean by Buddhism?' he continued. 'And in what way do you wish to preserve it? Buddhism is not its institutions, its traditions or even its culture. Rather, it is a spirit and a way of life. To preserve Buddhism is to preserve this spirit in a life of peace, compassion and wisdom. So what is important is not the number of temples that exist but how they are run.'

He then spoke about the 'enemy'. Were we trying to love our

enemy or not? Did we try to see them from a new perspective? In the Vietnamese war, thousands of Buddhists were harassed and killed by both sides. Many should be praised for the non-violent spirit of Buddhism they demonstrated. In the mid-1960s six Buddhists were killed when working to reconstruct homes for refugees. Their spirit was, 'We promise never to hate those who kill us, never to use violence to answer violence. Even if the antagonists see us as enemies and kill us, we recall our pledge that people, whatever their origin, never are our enemies.' He finished, 'The most dangerous threat is the one inside our minds. The real reason for the decline in Buddhism is not other ideologies but that Buddhists are not acting in the true spirit of their faith.'

In the discussion that followed, the monk was forced to defend his position. Most who spoke were monks, *bhikkhus*. The head monk of the temple said that he had come to believe that non-violence was not always possible, although desirable. Another claimed that Buddhism was neither totally for violence nor non-violence and asserted, rather at a tangent, that all the wars in the world were started by religions that believed in creation, absolving Buddhism of starting any war. When he then asserted that Buddhist monks had not killed Tamils but had only been killed by Tamils, another pointed out that Hindu priests had also been killed. The head monk, as if to deflect criticism, insisted that the monks in Sri Lanka were not racist or violent but added that he was certainly not convinced that an action programme based on non-violence would work.

Non-violence: the Buddhist ideal

The Thai monk was drawing on the Pāli textual tradition. There are some wonderfully inspirational narratives in the texts concerning non-violence, the *Kakacūpama Sutta* (The Discourse of the Parable of the Saw), for instance. It begins with humour that is almost slapstick. A woman is known for her calm and non-violence. Her maid, Kali, senses that this may only be skin deep and decides to test her. So she starts by being late to work. At first she is chastised verbally but, when the maid tests her further by arriving later and later, the reputedly calm woman eventually lashes out with a rolling pin and hits the maid on the head. Whereupon, the maid promptly goes into the town showing her bruises, ruining the reputation of her mistress. The Buddha then gives his monastic hearers a mantra-like principle to use in the face of the violence and verbal abuse that was present in Indian society at that time and which they might encounter and it is this:

Neither will our minds become perverted, nor will we utter evil speech, but kindly and compassionate will we dwell with a mind of friendliness, and void of hatred.

Most challenging is the extent to which this is to be taken. After describing a number of practical situations where such a mindset would be necessary, the Buddha ends with this:

Monks, as low-down thieves might carve one limb by limb with a double-handed saw, yet even then whoever sets his mind at enmity, he, for this reason, is not a doer of my teaching. Herein, monks, you should train yourselves thus: Neither will our minds become perverted . . . void of hatred.[1]

The monk, Punna, whom I mentioned in Chapter 2 took this to heart in his determination to act non-violently if provoked in the hostile Sunaparanta. We are not told what actually happens to Punna. There is no doubt, though, that his answers were intended to be an example to Buddhists, particularly those who had renounced. The mind has to be trained, in meditation, to think in non-violent ways, so that, when provocation arises, it will not lash out.

In keeping with these texts, Buddhism is often represented as a religious tradition that is utterly non-violent. A text that has become iconic is:

All tremble at violence
All fear death;
Comparing (others) with oneself
One should not kill or cause to kill.[2]

Similar to it is this one:

'As I (am) so (are) these. As (are) these, so (am) I'. Comparing himself (with others), he should not kill or cause to kill.[3]

Ideally, war and violence are always unwholesome within Buddhism. They are seen to be fuelled by hatred and the wish to kill. They generate hatred in the conquered and those involved risk serious karmic consequences.

Is non-violence possible?

Nevertheless, the dilemma of the Sri Lankan monks at the Naga Vihāra was a real one. Could the violence Sri Lanka was facing be ended purely by non-violent means? Wasn't the terrorist threat just too great? As the preceding chapters have shown, I was never in violence-neutral territory, divorced from conflict, during the time I lived in Sri Lanka. In the first few months, the violence was at a distance from where I lived in Colombo, although Tamil friends kept me well aware that there were killings and human rights abuses in the north and east, perpetrated by both the government and the militant groups. By the end of my first year, however, terrorist bombs and killings had come further south. And they continued throughout the time I lived in Sri Lanka. I have already mentioned several instances of the terrorist action of the LTTE, the gory, targeted killings of the JVP and the eventual backlash against the JVP from paramilitary groups linked to the state. I became familiar with curfews, an army presence on the streets and news of lifeless bodies in the streets.

For instance, in June 1988, the JVP, in an attempt to deter people from voting in elections for the Southern Provincial Council, threatened to kill the first five people at every voting centre. Directives such as these had happened before and continued afterwards. By November of that year, there was a curfew every night and foreign tourists were being advised to go home. The Presidential Election in December 1988 was accompanied by numerous killings, the closure of shops and offices and, again, curfews. The violence continued throughout 1989. In February, while I was meditating at Nilambe, ten people were killed by the JVP in Kandy, the nearest town. Three had been bus drivers who had broken a JVP-initiated strike. The others had been supporters of political parties the JVP considered traitorous. A month later, I was near Kandy again, to attend a Christian conference on 'The Sri Lankan Search for a Liberating Spirituality'. Some participants did not arrive because another bus driver had been killed and all buses had been stopped. The conference then concentrated on what kind of spirituality was possible when so many Sri Lankans were forced to sleep away from their homes for fear of the JVP or the military, or where one could not travel without fear that the driver or the passengers would be killed. Months later, I gave a presentation on women in Buddhism, again in Kandy, at Satyodaya, a Christian centre that housed a multi-faith community, which worked in nearby villages and with the people of the hill country. By this time the military were in the process of eliminating the JVP, matching the JVP in brutality and barbarism. To instil fear, on the morning of my talk, a gory necklace of severed heads had been placed around the roundabout at the entry to the university at Peradeniya. The closest I came to seeing the violence take place, though, was the time Tessa Bartholomeusz, and I went to Kataragama.

The new President elected in 1988, Premadasa, eventually ejected the IPKF and attempted peace talks with the LTTE. These broke down after a horrific LTTE-instigated programme of violence in the east of the country. The next Eelam War began and violence continued while I was researching my doctorate. It did not end after I left in 1993. In January 1996, for instance, a lorry loaded with explosives was rammed into the Central Bank in downtown Colombo by LTTE militants, killing up to 90 and injuring many more. Violence against Tamils was also endemic. For instance, in Trincomalee, in April 2006, government troops opened fire on innocent civilians after some members of the military had been killed by claymore mines. As I put the last touches to this book, during a further visit to Sri Lanka, the war is over but the conflict may not be and the total cost has been enormous. People of all religions and ethnic groups – Sinhala, Tamil, Muslim, Buddhist, Hindu and Christian – have been victims. But people of all religions have also been implicated in the conflict. The situation cries out for strategies of reconciliation.

Understanding violence

That the war has been ended in Sri Lanka through military force might seem to justify the questions of the Sri Lankan monks at the Naga Vihāra and to vindicate the view of those who suggested that violence, even in a predominantly Buddhist country, is sometimes necessary. I am not convinced that this is so but will leave the question to political analysts. The question I would like to reflect on is whether it is possible to reconcile what I have said so far about the attitude of the Buddhist texts towards violence and the violent course history has taken in countries such as Sri Lanka, which has been fed by the waters of Buddhism for centuries. I believe it is. Or rather, I believe Buddhism offers profound and relevant tools for the understanding of why violence arises and develops, tools that can shed light on both the war in Sri

Lanka and conflict in other parts of the world. For Buddhism gives us much more than a directive to train our minds and hearts in non-violent ways. It grapples with the roots of violence.

The Buddha's awareness of violence

As I mentioned in Chapter 1, so interested was I in this topic that I chose to do my MA dissertation on what the early Buddhist texts said about violence and disruption in society. First, I found that the texts were filled with references to violence. The Buddha lived in a time of violence – violence between competing monarchies, violence in the penal system, violence from bands of criminals – and the texts describe these. For instance, this is the kind of punishment that was meted out by kings at the time of the Buddha:

> Kings, having arrested such a one, deal out various punishments; they lash him with whips and they lash him with canes and they lash him with rods, and they cut off his hand . . . his foot . . . his hand and his foot . . . his ear . . . and they give him the 'gruel-pot' punishment . . . the 'shell-tonsure' punishment . . . 'Rahu's mouth' . . . the 'fire-garland' . . . the 'flaming hand' . . . etc.[4]

The Buddha is presented in the Pāli texts as an adviser to kings, in which context he was not shy of using military metaphors to press home spiritual points. To Pasenadi, King of Kosala, for instance, he speaks of the value of gifts and uses as an illustration what the king would do if a noble yet untrained and timid youth was to arrive when contending armies were massing, asking to fight.[5] On the evidence of the Pāli texts, the historical Buddha was neither ignorant of nor indifferent to political realities and the violence connected with them. The horrific story of a state falling into anarchy given in the *Cakkavatti Sīhanāda Sutta* is another example. As I pointed out in my MA dissertation, however, it was not only the violence inherent within political realities that he was aware of but also violence within the brahmanical sacrificial system, violence in the extreme self-mortification that some itinerant holy men practised, violence in the economic order and verbal violence between different religious leaders, described in the text in this way:

> Now there are ... certain recluses and Brahmins who are clever, subtle, experienced in controversy, hair splitters, who go about, one would think, breaking into pieces by their wisdom the speculations of their adversaries.[6]

All these forms of violence, the Buddha condemned. And he condemned them for at least two reasons: they led individual people away from the goal of *nibbāna*; they caused anguish to human beings and havoc within society. I have already stressed that greed, hatred and delusion are seen by Buddhists as the three poisons that cause our pain. Sometimes *sarambha* is added to these. It means 'accompanied by violence'. It is a defilement that flows from the three poisons, with the same consequence of leading people away from the goal of the Buddhist path.[7] Acting violently not only harms others. It harms oneself. Sometimes the Buddha, in the texts, is seen appealing to this principle with methods that medieval Christianity knew well – the citing of the tortures of hell:

> Brahmin youth, here some woman or man is one that makes onslaught on creatures, is cruel, bloody-handed, intent on injuring and killing, and without mercy to living creatures. Because of that deed, accomplished thus, firmly held thus, he, at the breaking up of the body after dying, arises in the sorrowful way, the bad bourn, the Downfall, the Niraya (one of the hells).[8]

In the iconography of Buddhism, just as in Christianity, hells feature. In 1993, when I visited a *vihāra* near Matara in southern Sri Lanka, I was surprised to find, in a gallery close to the shrine room, modern, life-size, three-dimensional demonstrations of what happened in the hells to those who acted immorally. In older *vihāras*, this was done through murals. Some extremely graphic ones can be found at the *Aluvihāra* in Sri Lanka, the temple in the centre of the country where the Pāli Canon is said to have been written down in the first century BCE. One shows the punishment for people who kill head lice!

The importance of realism

The Buddha's context was different from our context in the twenty-first century but the emotive feel of the violence that was present in the Buddha's time has always struck me as similar to that of our own time. The torture techniques used in Iraq by the Americans, for instance, were not so different from those used in the Buddha's day. In grappling with the reality of violence and its roots, the hallmark of the Buddha's method, as far as we can glimpse it from the texts, was realism. For instance, it is not denied that states need armies capable of defending their citizens against aggression. Among the duties of a king mentioned in the *Cakkavatti Sīhanāda Sutta*, together with giving the means to live to the poor, is to protect the army and there is a controversial conversation in one text when the Buddha seems to endorse a king who successfully defends his nation against an aggressor.[9] It is texts such as these that have been used by some Sinhala Buddhists in Sri Lanka to justify a military solution to the ethnic conflict and no doubt they were in the minds of some of the monks who listened to their visitor from Thailand at the Naga Vihāra. Buddhists, in practice, have never been completely non-violent. Buddhist countries have neither been without armies nor systems of punishment. To recognize this is to be realistic. To recognize the difficulty inherent in trying to put into practice the radical non-violent ideal in Buddhism is also to be realistic.

One popular reaction to extreme violence whether perpetrated by an individual or group is, 'How can any human do that?' Of suicide bombers we exclaim, 'How can humans get to the point where they could blow up themselves and others?' Of those in Nazi Germany who supported Hitler's genocide against the Jews, we cry, 'How could ordinary men – loving husbands and fathers – carry on with their everyday life and at the same time send thousands of Jews to their deaths?' It is as though the violent ones are placed in a sub-human category, far away from us, the non-violent ones.[10]

Buddhism claims that we will never understand violence if we stay at this level. Buddhism's realism has taught me at least two things in connection with violence.[11] First, it has convinced me that violence is to be expected in our world. Second, it has taught me that the perpetrators of violence are not aberrations within the human race. They are people like me and you, who are caught in their own prisons of greed, hatred and delusion.

There is a telling story in the texts about the Buddha's enlightenment. When he awoke to the truth about existence, he first of all refused to teach, believing that no one would understand what he would try to say. The view of existence that he had seen and the path towards the eradication of pain were too difficult, too counter-intuitive we might say now. At that point a heavenly being comes to him, fearing that the world will miss the teaching of a Buddha. He pleads with the Buddha to teach. 'There are people with less defilements, who will understand,' he points out, 'Look with your Buddha eye at the world and you will see that it is so.' The Buddha realizes the truth of what he is being told and agrees to teach.

It is the reason why the Buddha could have been wary of communicating his newly gained wisdom that has interested me. According to the texts, one of the things that the Buddha saw at his enlightenment was that people are reborn because they have not destroyed egotistical craving. He saw them passing from life to life because of this, driven by their wish to preserve the 'self' from death. As I have shown, this is how Buddhists see our human condition. Inherent within this is the potential for violence. It is simply part of our unenlightened human condition. Deep within the Buddhist texts is a recognition that only a few will truly understand the Buddha's teaching, as this verse from the Dhammapada shows, echoing the Buddha's fear at his enlightenment:

The world has become blind; few see here.
A few go to heaven
Like a bird released from a net.[12]

If this is accepted – that only a few will truly understand the teachings of a religion such as Buddhism – we should not be surprised when violence arises, even among Buddhists. For Buddhists are people who are still on the path, who are only in the process of eradicating the greed, hatred and delusion within them. Enlightenment is not something to be plucked off a tree. It is hard-won.

I am not speaking here of an acceptance of violence or a hardening of the heart towards it but of an understanding that violence is to be expected in a world where relatively few have ears to hear the message of the Buddha or indeed the non-violent message of other religions, Christianity included. The corollary of this is that transforming violence is a long and arduous task, when we, the unenlightened attempt it, as the history of the conflict in places such as Israel/Palestine show.

Analysing causes

The second thing that Buddhism has taught me flows from this. It is that those who perpetrate violence are not to be scorned as aberrations. They do not arise through chance. They are formed by conditions, by external and internal causal factors. Crime and mystery novelist Ruth Rendell, in her book, *The Crocodile Bird*, gives a chilling example of this. One of its central characters is the beautiful and intelligent Eve Beck, who cloisters herself and her daughter away from the world and, over a period of 12 years, kills three men who threaten her security. Eventually the reader learns that Eve, when she was a promising student in Oxford, was brutally raped by three men when she hitched a lift from Heathrow Airport. Illness and prolonged psychiatric treatment followed. And she never completed her degree. She emerged from the experience with a daughter and an almost fanatical wish to avoid engagement with the world. She is eventually convicted and imprisoned. Rendell implicitly asks the question: would Eve have killed if she herself had not been victimized and traumatized? The novel presents Eve as both murderer and the victim of violence.[13]

When Buddhism points to the importance of conditioning factors, it is not advocating a form of fatalism. It does not argue that we are heirs to our conditioning and cannot escape it. Rendell was not putting forward fatalism either. She shows this through the figure of the daughter, Lisa. Lisa also is tempted at one point to kill, just as she knows her mother has done, when she finds that her identity is threatened by a man in a way similar to Eve's experience. She is in danger of becoming her mother. But she does not so become, finding a far less dramatic way to solve the changes in youthful relationships. The mother's imbalance is not repeated in the child. Similarly, Buddhism is adamant that we can break free of our conditioning if we are aware of what is influencing us. When a person or a community is unable to do this, though, again Buddhism teaches us that we should not be surprised, although we may grieve.

We should not be surprised and we should look at causal factors. As I have made clear, cause and condition are central to the Buddhist world view and path. They are central to the Four Noble Truths and should be central to the Buddhist's analytical method. For Buddhism calls for an analytical, empirical attitude when we are dealing with anything to do with human life, including the question of violence. In the case of an incidence of violence, reflective Buddhists might suggest questions such as these: How did violence arise in this situation? What were the conditioning factors? If the violence is due to greed, hatred or anger, what triggered it? Was it the wish to protect the identity of a group? Was it because contempt had been shown towards oneself or one's community? Was it because, when self was compared with 'other', jealousy or a sense of victimhood arose – an emotion that the Pāli would call *māna*, the tendency to compare self with others? Or was it connected with another Pāli concept, *diṭṭhi*, which concerns the danger of dogmatic or speculative views, the danger of saying that this alone is truth and all else is falsehood.[14] Then again, was it because an arrogant state had ripped the means of livelihood from the poor?

Buddhism has never declared that violence in society is due purely to the poisons in the minds of the perpetrators. The already mentioned *Cakkavatti Sīhanāda Sutta* illustrates this. So does the *Kūṭadanta Sutta*. This tells a myth within a myth. The inner myth tells the story of King Wide Realm, whose country is shot through with discontent. People are afraid to venture far outside their houses for fear of violence. The king goes to a holy man for advice, believing that the solution is to hold a huge sacrifice for the good of his land. The advice he is actually given, though, is this:

Whoever there be in the king's realm who devote themselves to keeping cattle and the farm, to them let his majesty give food and seed corn. Whosoever there be in the king's realm who devote themselves to trade to them let his majesty give capital. Whosoever there be in the king's realm who devote themselves to government service, to them let his majesty give wages and food. Then those men, following each his own business, will no longer harass the realm; the king's revenue will go up; the country will be quiet and at peace; and the populace pleased with one another and happy, dancing their children in their arms, will dwell with open doors.[15]

In other words, he is advised to create greater economic justice in his land. The cause of the disruption in the kingdom is seen to be the king's blindness and greediness not inherent criminality in the populace.

Poverty caused by unjust governance at national or international level is still a cause of conflict. Another, often unrecognized, key to understanding conflict, I would suggest, is 'contempt'.[16] Anger, resentment and violence very often have their roots in the conviction that contempt is being directed towards one's ethnic, linguistic or religious identity. I can remember a conversation with Lily de Silva, Professor of Buddhist Studies and Pāli at Peradeniya University, in which she said the main cause of conflict was clinging to identity. When a community believes that it is viewed with contempt, the defence of identity, self-respect and dignity becomes all important – and violent or conflictual ways of defence can easily be judged the only option. In Sri Lanka, the experience of contempt has fed the attitude some Buddhists have towards what they, rightly in some cases, judge to be 'unethical conversions' by Christian groups. Their accusation is that Christians are bribing poverty-stricken Buddhists and Hindus to become Christians through promises of material benefits such as schooling. Churches have been attacked because of this and legislation to prohibit forced conversion has been tabled, but not so far passed, in the Sri Lankan Parliament. The roots of this, according to my doctoral research and subsequent work, goes back to the nineteenth century when Sri Lanka was under British rule, and a Buddhist Revival arose in antagonistic response to the evangelistic endeavours of Christian missionaries.

In the course of my research, I came across this record of a conversation between an Anglican Bishop and a Buddhist monk in 1863, written by the former:

> They were moved when I said that I came to them (the Buddhist monks) as the teachers of the people, feeling sure that if they could be convinced that my Religion was true they would wish to teach it instead of their own. They told me that nothing had more turned them against Christianity than finding themselves treated with marked contempt by its professors.[17]

This and other archival evidence has convinced me that the eventual cause of antagonism between Christians and Buddhists during the British colonial period was not that Christians preached Christianity, or that they gained some converts – these could have been accommodated. It was not the differences between Christian and Buddhist belief and practice – these could have been debated. It was that the Christian missionaries showed contempt towards what Buddhists believed and practised. They judged Buddhism to be pessimistic, nihilistic and in league with the devilish. The consequence was that some Buddhists, in defence of their self-respect and identity, threw away their previous wish for non-violent co-existence with Christians and adopted the competitive methods of the missionaries, which led to a form of verbal violence that did justice to neither religion.

The mind and its devices: constructing realities

I will say more about the consequences of this in the next chapter. Here, it is enough to point out that my research into current Buddhist–Christian mistrust in Sri Lanka has been helped by Buddhism's emphasis on cause. Both my understanding of this Buddhist–Christian mistrust and of violence has also been helped by the Buddhist concept of *papañca*, as described by a scholar monk called Bhikkhu Ñānananda.[18] The word is often translated as 'proliferation', although it has also been translated as 'obsessions'.[19] One discourse, the *Madhupiṇḍika Sutta* (Discourse of the Honey Ball), declares *papañca* to be the root of taking up weapons and the defeat of *papañca* as the way to end such violence.[20]

The 'proliferation' of *papañca* refers to the proliferation of sense impressions and thoughts. As I wrote in my MA dissertation, it is, 'a tendency for the conceptual process to run riot'.[21] Ñānananda's contribution concerns the internal dynamics of this. The *Madhupiṇḍika Sutta* states, using Ñānananda's translation:

> Visual consciousness, brethren, arises because of eye and visible forms; the meeting of the three is sensory impingement; because of sensory impingement arises feeling; what one feels, one perceives; what one perceives, one reasons about; what one reasons about, one turns into *papañca*, due to that *papañca-saññā-sankhā* assail him in regard to visible forms cognizable by the eye belonging to the past, the future and the present.[22]

From this, using linguistic analysis, Ñānananda concludes that the process involves deliberate activity up to the point of *papañca* but, after this, the subject becomes the object. The person reasoning becomes the victim of his sense awareness and perceptions. Ñānananda writes:

> Like the legendary tiger which devoured the magician who restored it to life out of its skeletal bones, the concepts and

linguistic conventions overwhelm the worldling who evolved them. At the final and crucial stage of sense-perception, the concepts are, as it were, invested with an objective quality.[23]

The breeding ground for this is a mind that is still governed by such things as craving, *māna* (the tendency to measure oneself against others), *diṭṭhi* (clinging to views and opinions) and ego-consciousness. For such a mind, the conscious and unconscious touchstone at each point of awareness and thought is the self and its needs. *Papañca* is nurtured in this atmosphere and, according to Ñānananda, it has something to do with language. In trying to explain the process, I wrote this:

The conventions of language enter near the beginning of the process of sense perception, at the point where feeling gives rise to mental activity and concepts. The mind, if unchecked, will attempt to place order on its feelings through language. This language immediately introduces the dualism of subject and object, subject and feeling. The 'I' enters with 'I feel aversion' or 'I feel attraction' or 'I like this' or 'I don't like this' . . . What seems to happen after that is that language takes on a dynamism of its own. Concepts proliferate and leave the empirical behind, under the driving force of *taṇhā*, *māna* and *diṭṭhi*. For instance, the observation, 'I feel aversion' might lead to further thoughts such as: I am right to feel aversion . . . Therefore, the object is inherently worthy of aversion . . . So the object must be got rid of . . . I cannot survive unless the object is annihilated from my sphere of vision and feeling . . . It is my duty to annihilate this for my sake and the sake of others.[24]

In my MA writing I drew a parallel with Immanuel Kant, who also doubted that pure reason could extend our knowledge of reality, because the mind was predisposed to find the unconditional unity that humans called God. The concept of *papañca* has helped me to see that humans can become the victims of themselves when they are unaware that the first steps of their argument or thought process might be rooted in selfishness or subjective thoughts, 'I do not like this' or 'I cannot live without this.' If Ñānananda is right, such thoughts, when they have proliferated, can lead to war, genocide or torture, with the perpetrator unaware of the full horror of what has been unleashed or that his or her thought processes were not based on reason but were flawed from the beginning. The 'reality' that was perceived was a constructed reality, which then took on a life of its own.

When I first read Ñānananda's work, he made sense to me, particularly when I looked at humanity's ability to create and deploy nuclear weapons. Their supporters are convinced that such weapons are a reasonable mode of deterrence. With Ñānananda in mind, I asked myself, 'But what kind of thought process has led to this? What was the basic flawed principle?' How was the 'reality' of the supporters of nuclear weapons constructed? Surely, in nuclear and biological weapons, humans have created something out of their greed that now makes them victims. In the light of Buddhist wisdom, it might be true to say that nuclear weapons are horrific expressions of the tendency for greed and hatred in the human mind to proliferate and become monstrous.

To summarize the first part of this chapter, therefore, my journey into Buddhism has taught me that Buddhism holds out an ideal that is non-violent. Only non-violent methods truly lead to benefit for self and others. Yet, it is also realistic, recognizing that violence is an inevitable part of a world still in the grip of greed, hatred and delusion, both in the minds of individuals and institutions such as the state. And in its analysis of this situation it offers radical tools for understanding how violent tendencies arise and how they should be understood.

Eradicating violence

Does Buddhism then hold out any hope that violent tendencies can be eradicated? The answer must be a resounding Yes. But there is no single key. We would not expect this from the realism and pragmatism of the Buddha. And no utopia is promised. Buddhism has no concept of an everlasting state that is filled with peace and justice. This world is part of *saṃsāra* and all within *saṃsāra* is impermanent. Yet, within Buddhist literature there are numerous examples of violent people and situations that change. In the *Cakkavatti Sīhanāda Sutta*, the solution, unlike the problem, comes from the bottom upwards. A group of people, suddenly made aware of the bestiality of what they are doing, retreat into the jungle and the mountains to exist on wild fruits and roots. After this they return, renewed, to greet their neighbour as friend rather than foe. Creating distance between violence and the self and allowing time to reflect both help to create change. Then there is the story of Ven. Angulimala, a revered follower of the Buddha, who enters Buddhist story as a multiple murderer. When he first appears in the texts, he wears, as a necklace, the fingers of those he has killed and terrorizes his neighbourhood. An encounter with the Buddha, in which the Buddha uses paranormal powers to convince him that he must change, causes conversion.

The Buddha is also shown using reason in a story that is found in the commentary on the Dhammapada. I use the account of it given by John McConnell, conflict resolution trainer. The Sakyas and Koliyas, two groups in north-east India, live on opposite sides of the river Rohini, which they use for irrigation. They have had a history of co-operation but, when drought comes, co-operation turns to mutual suspicion. Eventually each side prepares for war, not so much because of the water, but because of the insults that had been hurled between the two. The Buddha is eventually called in. He was, after all, from the clan of the Sakyas, and the dialogue goes something like this:

The Buddha: How much is water worth, Great King?
The King: Very little, reverend Sir.
The Buddha: How much are warriors worth, Great King?
The King: Warriors are beyond price, Reverend Sir.
The Buddha: It is not fitting that because of a little water you should destroy warriors who are beyond price.
There is then silence. The Buddha adds:
Were I not present today you would set flowing a river of blood. You have acted in a most unbecoming manner. You live in enmity, indulging in the five kinds of hatred. I live free from hatred.[25]

The two parties then draw back from conflict.

Not all change comes as quickly as in these examples in Buddhist sources. Theravāda Buddhism has always stressed the need for gradual training, a training that starts where people are. Mahāyāna Buddhism would call this skilful means.

The advanced part of this gradual training is the kind of mind training that I described in the last chapter, most particularly guarding the doors of the senses – watching one's reactions to contact between the senses and the world, and noticing when they are governed by such things as greed or fears connected with the self. Meditations on impermanence can also help. In a sermon at Poson, the June Full Moon Day in Sri Lanka, when the coming of Buddhism to Sri Lanka is remembered, I can remember one monk stressing that a meditation on death eradicates violent tendencies. If humans are able truly to imagine themselves dead or dying, the monk implied, then their greeds, worries and angers disappear. They are relativized in the face of the inevitability of decay and impermanence.

Empathy and interbeing

The ability to stand in another's shoes is also a step along the path to non-violence. As I have shown, Buddhist ethics is rooted in empathy. One avoids killing because all living beings feel pain and desire happiness as much as oneself. Feeling this at an emotive level stays our hands from violence. Some Mahāyāna Buddhists take this further through placing emphasis on the fact that we are interdependent with everything else. Thich Nhat Hanh, a Vietnamese Zen master popular in the West, speaks of interbeing rather than interdependence, and is founder of the Order of Interbeing. The Order encourages its members in 14 mindfulness trainings which include:

Ist Training

Aware of the suffering caused by fanaticism and intolerance, I am determined not to be idolatrous about or bound to any doctrine, theory or ideology, even Buddhist ones. Buddhist teachings are guiding means to help me learn to look deeply and to develop my understanding and compassion. They are not doctrines to fight, kill or die for.

12th Training – Reverence for Life

Aware that much suffering is caused by war and conflict, I am determined to cultivate non-violence, understanding and com-passion in my daily life, to promote peace education, mindful mediations and reconciliation, within families, communities, nations and the world. I am determined not to kill and not to let others kill. I will diligently practice deep looking with my Sangha (community) to discover better ways to protect life and prevent war.[26]

Nhat Hanh takes empathy and the recognition of interbeing almost to its limits in a poem he wrote at the time of the Vietnamese boat people. Introducing the poem, *Call me by my true names*, Nhat Hanh claims it has three characters: a 12-year-old girl, who throws herself into the sea after being raped by a pirate as she is crossing the Gulf of Siam in the Vietnamese War, the pirate, born in a poor village, uneducated, who raped the girl, and Thich Nhat Hanh, angry at the event but realizing that he could have been that sea pirate if he had been born in the same circumstances. So he writes in the poem:

> I am the twelve-year-old girl,
> refugee on a small boat,
> who throws herself into the ocean
> After being raped by a sea pirate.
> and I am the pirate,
> my heart not yet capable
> of seeing and loving.

He ends:

> Please call me by my true names,
> so I can wake up,
> and so the door of my heart
> can be left open,
> the door of compassion.[27]

In this poem, Thich Nhat Hanh identifies with both the girl and the pirate, who in effect murders the girl through raping her. The pirate's deed is not justified nor the consequences minimized. But the conclusion of Nhat Hanh was that, if the circumstances conditioning him had been different, he could have been the pirate or the girl. When I have used this poem in teaching, especially when the students are Christian, the usual reaction has been one of incredulity. How could a socially engaged person, aware of the exploitation of women, express empathy with a rapist! Nhat Hanh might say, 'I can see your point. But I would not re-write the poem. We are as interlinked with this uneducated sea pirate as with the saints of the world and should not withhold compassion.'

I have sometimes said that Buddhism offers two messages concerning the transformation of violence. The first is that both empathy and reason are crucial, empathy to stand in the shoes of the other, reason to ask people the right questions and to address the causes of conflict. The second is the encouraging and devel-oping of fearlessness and freedom from worry for self, gained through mental culture. The kind of empathy that Nhat Hanh encourages is hard to develop in some conflict situations, par-ticularly where there are competitions in comparative suffering, each side claiming that it is they who have suffered most at the hands of the terrorist 'other'. In Palestine/Israel there is such a competition. Many Jews of Israel believe they are suffering most as the victims of terrorist attacks from Palestine and the unwill-ingness of some Muslim states to recognize the right of Israel to exist. Many Palestinians believe, on the other hand, that it is they who have suffered the most, turned out of their villages in the initial years of state-formation in Israel, cut off from their livelihoods by the current barrier wall and denied freedom of movement in a land that once was theirs. A similar situation con-tinues to exist in Sri Lanka, even after the war has ended. Peace, as one Hindu Tamil social activist told me, will only come when the Sinhala people can grieve for and commemorate members of the LTTE and the Tamil civilians who have lost their lives in the conflict, and the Tamil people can grieve for and commemo-rate the members of the military and the Sinhala civilians who have similarly lost their lives. In other words, peace will come when people on both sides of the conflict can give up the victim mentality and step into the shoes of the 'other' to recognize the reasons why Tamil and Sinhala young people could have been persuaded to join the LTTE or the army respectively, to become killers and then victims, when death came to meet them. Such wisdom has become part of conflict-transformation strategy. But it has a religious root.

Notes

1 *Majjhima Nikāya*, vol. I 129, I. B. Horner (trans.), 1987 *The Middle Length Sayings*, Oxford: Pāli Text Society, pp. 159–66). See Elizabeth J. Harris, 1994, *Violence and Disruption in Society: A Study of Early Buddhist Texts*, Kandy: Buddhist Publication Society, p. 4.

2 Dhammapada, v. 129, K. R. Norman, 1997, *The Word of the Doctrine*, Oxford: Pāli Text Society, p. 20.

3 *Sutta Nipāta*, v. 705, K. R. Norman (trans.), 2000, *The Group of Discourses*, Oxford: Pāli Text Society, p. 92.

4 *Mahādukkhakhandha Sutta* (Greater Discourse on the Stems of Anguish), *Majjhima Nikāya*, vol. I 87, I. B. Horner, 1987, *The Middle Length Sayings* 115, quoted in Elizabeth J. Harris, 1994, *Violence and Disruption and Society*, p. 6.

5 *Saṃyutta Nikāya*, vol. I 97, quoted in Harris, 1994, *Violence and Disruption in Society*, p. 5.

6 *Kassapa Sīhanāda Sutta*, *Dīgha Nikāya*, vol. I 162, T. W. Rhys Davids (trans.), 1977 (1899), *Dialogues of the Buddha*, Part I: 224, quoted in Harris, 1994, *Violence and Disruption*, p. 8.

7 *Aṅguttara Nikāya*, vol. II 191 (A discourse with Bhaddiya) quoted in Harris, 1994, *Violence and Disruption*, p.14.

8 *Cūḷakammavibhanga Sutta*, *Majjhima Nikāya*, vol. III 303 (Horner, 1990, *Middle Length Sayings*, vol. III: 206), quoted in Harris, 1994, *Violence and Disruption*, p. 15

9 See Harris, 1994, *Violence and Disruption*, pp. 18–19.

10 See also Elizabeth J. Harris, 2006, 'What Can Buddhism Offer a Violent World?', *Interreligious Insight*, vol. 4, no. 1, pp. 54–62.

11 I first spoke about this in a paper given at the Sion Centre for Dialogue and Encounter, February 2007 on 'Understanding Violence: How can Buddhism help?'.

12 Dhammapada, v. 174 (Norman, 1997, *The Word of the Doctrine*, p. 26)

13 Ruth Rendell, 1993, *The Crocodile Bird*, London: Hutchinson.

14 Harris, *Violence and Disruption*, p. 32.

15 *Kūṭadanta Sutta, Dīgha Nikāya*, vol. I 135 (T. W. Rhys Davids (trans.), 1977, *Dialogues of the Buddha*, Part I, Oxford: Pāli Text Society, p. 176.

16 See Elizabeth J. Harris, 2007, 'Transforming Conflict: Can Religion Help?' in John O'Grady and Peter Scherle (eds), *Ecumenics from the Rim: Explorations in Honour of John D'Arcy May*, Berlin: Lit Verlag, pp. 387–94.

17 Bishop Claughton writing to the Revd E. Hawkins from Colombo, 13 January 1863 (Ceylon Letters, vol. II USPG Archives), quoted in Harris, 2006, *Theravāda Buddhism and the British Encounter*, p. 189.

18 Bhikkhu Ñāṇananda, 1971, *Concept and Reality in Early Buddhist Thought*, Kandy: Buddhist Publication Society.

19 I. B. Horner's translation renders it in this way in the translation below.

20 *Madhupiṇḍika Sutta, Majjhima Nikāya*, vol. I, 109–10 (I. B. Horner, 1987, *Middle Length Sayings*, p. 143.

21 Harris, 1994, *Violence and Disruption*, p. 28.

22 *Majjhima Nikāya*, Vol. I 111–12, quoted in Harris, *Violence and Disruption*, pp. 28–9.

23 Ñāṇananda, *Concept and Reality*, p. 6, quoted in Harris, 1994, *Violence and Disruption*, p. 29.

24 Harris, 1994, *Violence and Disruption*, p. 30.

25 See John A. McConnell, 2001, *Mindful Mediation: A Handbook for Buddhist Peacemakers*, Bangkok: Buddhist Research Institute, Mahachula University, pp. 315–25.

26 See www.orderofinterbeing.org.

27 From Thich Nhat Hanh, 1999, *Call Me by My True Names: The Collected Poems of Thich Nhat Hanh*, Berkeley, California: Parallax Press.

6

Inter Faith Relations

At the end of my first year in Sri Lanka, in summer 1987, I was asked to write an article for *Discernment*, a journal of the Committee for Relationships with People of Other Faiths (CRPOF) of the British Council of Churches (BCC), as they then were. It included these words:

> After a year, I am now asking myself what I have learnt about the possibilities for encounter, action, trust and, yes, dialogue between different faiths in Sri Lanka. Have I understood what the challenge is? Is it being taken up? Two themes have dominated my reflections: that opportunities for inter faith understanding can be destroyed or created by social, economic and political realities; that sharing at the level of human hopes and fears – a dialogue of life – should precede dialogue about religious experience.

The two themes were rooted in my experiences during the first year. An early conversation with a Buddhist woman academic, Dr Hema Gunatileke, the woman who encouraged me to go to Bodh Gaya in my first year, set the tone for my thoughts on the first of these. When we met, I cannot remember using the word dialogue. She assumed, however, that that was what I had come for. One of the first things she said to me, therefore, was that she had to challenge my presence. In her view, she continued, those who wanted dialogue between faiths were usually from the West

– the dominant part of the world. Because of the power imbalance, therefore, dialogue could never be a meeting of equals, she insisted. She continued, 'Dialogue is usually domination. What begins as sharing often results in domination by the most powerful side.' All this was said in a friendly tone and we became friends. Nevertheless, it made me see that however much I insisted that I was the learner in Sri Lanka, some people, if they knew I was a Christian, would see me either as seeking to dominate or to convert Buddhists, simply because I was western and Christian.

Buddhist–Christian mistrust: its nineteenth-century roots

Christians make up about 7.5 per cent of the Sri Lankan population. Although archaeological evidence proves that there were Christians from the Church of the East in Sri Lanka from an early date, Christians in the country today trace their identity back to one of three western colonial rulers: Portuguese (1505–1656/8), Dutch (1656/8–1796) and British (1796–1948). Roman Catholics form the largest group within the Christian community. Among the Protestants, the Church of Ceylon (Anglican Communion), the Methodist Church and the Church of South India (found only among the Tamil community) are the largest denominations.

A key period in the history of Buddhist–Christian relations in the country was the nineteenth century, when Sri Lanka, then Ceylon, was under British rule. The significance of it was the reason why Aloysius Pieris suggested that I should examine it for a doctorate. It has proved such a fertile area that the study of it has expanded far beyond the doctorate itself. There is not enough space here to give a nuanced story. I have done this elsewhere and in the last chapter mentioned the contempt of the British evangelical missionaries as a factor in the animosity shown towards Christianity in the Buddhist Revival.[1] To cut a long story short, mistrust between Christians and Buddhists gained momentum when the new independent missionary societies, children of the Evangelical Revival in Britain, began to send missionaries to the island. Archival evidence shows that the Buddhist monastic community, at the beginning, generally sought a co-existence model of inter faith relations, namely one governed by respect and tolerance. The monastic community, having experienced Roman Catholicism under the Portuguese and the Dutch Reformed Church under the Dutch, was well aware that Christianity differed from Buddhism and no doubt some members felt hostility to it and were aware of folk stories that belittled Christianity.[2] In general terms, though, the monastic community preferred debate rather than polemic and respect between faiths rather than competition, although it is possible that there were regional differences, the extreme south of the country being more openly hostile. Their tolerance and respect was shown in hospitality. William Harvard, one of the first Wesleyan missionaries, wrote to his mother, with a note of surprise, that he had been allowed to preach in a Buddhist temple.[3] Other temples allowed the missionaries to stay overnight if they were travelling around the country. Scholar missionaries were given precious Pāli manuscripts and even taught Pāli. Robert Spence Hardy, another Wesleyan missionary, wrote retrospectively:

> They would have been willing to enter into an alliance with the servants of God, and would have had no hesitation in worshipping Jesus Christ if they (the missionaries) would have worshipped Buddha. According to their ideas, Jesus Christ was a good man, as Buddha was a good man; and if Buddha was only regarded as the best, what should hinder the formation of a compact between the two systems, that would have brought the whole of the Sinhalese people under one religious rule?[4]

Within Buddhism, incorporation of other beliefs while maintaining the supremacy of the Buddha, is a time-honoured tradition. So was courtesy to those holding other beliefs, going back at least to the third century BCE when the Buddhist Mauryan king, Asoka, in India, published rock and pillar edicts that advocated tolerance and respect between people of different beliefs. As the nineteenth century progressed, however, a shift in attitude took place. The wish for co-existence and tolerance receded, as the Buddhist monastic community realized that the missionaries were not going to reciprocate their courtesy but were bent on proselytizing. One of their first reactions to provocation by the missionaries was to send petitions to the Government requesting respect between faiths. When they did not receive a response, they realized that the Government was not going to intervene either. They were on their own, facing a threat to their identity, a threat to the *dhamma*, in the island for which they believed the Buddha had a special love. There is no doubt that those who had offered hospitality to the early British missionaries and had even taught them Pāli felt betrayed, especially when they became aware that missionary writing, as a means of proselytization, was representing Buddhism as pessimistic, morally impotent and idolatrous.

A sense of betrayal was felt quite early. It was 1805 when the first missionaries from the independent missionary societies arrived, sent by the London Missionary Society. Baptists arrived in 1812, Wesleyans in 1814 and Anglicans with the Church Missionary Society in 1818. As early as 1819, Daniel J. Gogerly wrote in the *School Report of the Methodist Mission* (Wesleyan Mission Press: Colombo) that Buddhism was seeking to re-establish itself in several parts of the south.[5]

After petitions to the Government failed, the monastic community compiled treatises, countering the accusations made by the missionaries against Buddhism, written on traditional ola leaves, since the missionaries would not allow the Buddhist community to use Christian printing presses. These were taken around the villages in order to strengthen Buddhists against the missionaries. When, in 1855 and 1862, the Buddhist community acquired printing presses, the point of outright confrontation was reached. Missionary methods, instead of converting the island to Christianity, in fact fuelled a full-blown Buddhist revival that empowered both lay and ordained Buddhists. In the 1860s and 1870s there were several high-profile debates between Buddhists and Christians, culminating in the Panadura Debate of 1873. The transcript of this internationalized the Sri Lankan Buddhist–Christian struggle, by attracting the attention of the founders of the Theosophical Society, Colonel Henry Olcott and Helena Blavatsky, who came to Sri Lanka in 1880, in order to stand alongside Buddhists against Christianity. They were followed by others.

The missionaries had judged the earlier conciliatory attitude of Buddhists to be the result of apathy, indifference to or overconfidence in their faith.[6] Why else did they not stand up for what they believed? In some ways they found the revival easier to deal with, because the Buddhist attitude to inter faith relations had, in defence, moved closer to their own. Wesleyan missionary, Thomas Moscrop, could declare in 1894 at a missionary meeting in Birmingham:

You have already made the inference, Buddhism is alive; but have you made the further inference, drawn by us on the field, that it is alive because Christianity has proved itself to be alive; that it has felt our grip and become alarmed, aggressive?[7]

The contempt shown by the missionaries towards Buddhist belief and practice was a key factor in this development. To those westerners who showed courtesy to Buddhism, courtesy was always returned.

The nineteenth-century missionaries were men and women of their time. They should not be judged by twenty-first-century standards. Yet, as I look back on this history, one of the most tragic elements of the process was the mutual demonization it led to. The missionaries, in their writings throughout the century, had accused Buddhism of fatalism, pessimism and nihilism, and of being intricately involved in devil worship through the 'devil dance', which today anthropologists would call exorcism, something not unfamiliar to Christianity. These accusations, in the course of the revival, were thrown back, in full measure, at Christianity. At the Panadura Debate, the main Buddhist protagonist attempted, through a literalist interpretation of the Bible, to prove that the God of the Christians was really a demon-like being. How else could Christians revere the murderer Moses or accept as God's son a person whose birth was accompanied by the culling of children?[8] Western theosophists who, after the debate, came to aid the revival supplemented this rhetoric. This is what Charles Leadbeater (1854–1934), who arrived in Sri Lanka from Britain in 1886, having resigned from the Anglican priesthood, wrote of the Christianity of the missionaries:

> It cannot live in peace with any other form of faith. It holds that there is but one saviour, but one inspired book, and but one little narrow grass-grown path that leads to heaven. Such a religion is necessarily uncompromising, unreasoning, aggressive and insolent. It has held all other creeds and forms in infinite contempt, divided the world into enemies and friends and amply verified that awful declaration of its founder, 'I come not to bring peace but a sword'.[9]

The dynamics of this nineteenth-century confrontation has not died. Throughout my time in Sri Lanka, mistrust between Buddhists and Christians easily flared up, the most common accusation against Christians being that they were involved in 'unethical conversions'. At a Sakyadhita conference held in Colombo in 1993, I was told that every small discussion group with Asian participants raised the issue of unethical conversions.

Then, when I was in Sri Lanka in 1999, this time as a member of an ecumenical group from Churches Together in Britain and Ireland, a Buddhist academic told the group that it was as though there was a cold war between religions in Sri Lanka. In the years following 1999, this led to a number of serious attacks on churches, sometimes led by Buddhist monks. In 2009, as I finish this book, tension between the two religions is still high.

Although the number of Buddhists involved in attacks on churches is miniscule and although Christians and Buddhists co-exist fairly peacefully in many parts of Sri Lanka, Christians who enter the country to seek dialogue with Buddhists and also Sri Lankan Christians with the same wish inevitably have to work against the backdrop of this turbulent history. Neither Christians nor Buddhists in Sri Lanka can stand outside it. Trust has had to be built up the hard way.

Contemporary Buddhist–Christian mistrust

During my time in Sri Lanka I faced this mistrust on several occasions. Usually, even when I said that I was a Christian, I was welcomed with the greatest of courtesy, as I hope the first chapter has shown. Yet I was also forced to realize that mistrust was not far below the surface. In early 1993, for instance, the Women's Commission of the Sri Lankan National Council of Churches asked me to invite some Buddhist women to speak at a conference the Commission was organizing on the issue of women and violence. I asked two women whom I had come to know through the Sri Lanka Sakyadhita Group. I was nervous and so were they. They eventually accepted because they knew me, and the session was an astounding success. They took the theme of meditation and mind-training, skirting the issue of violence against women that the conference was addressing. Yet, the main speaker, Kusuma Devendra, now Bhikkhunī Kusuma, spoke with such commitment that everyone was drawn to her. Sensing that the group was listening to her with respect, she was willing to answer the most challenging of questions. Afterwards, the two shared with me that they had been advised by Buddhist friends not to accept my invitation, because the Christian women might try to use them. As I drove with them to their next destination, one of them was radiant, saying that Buddhist and Christian women must co-operate and that I had a role in bringing the two groups together.

Later in the same year, however, when an international Sakyadhita Conference was held in Colombo, mistrust raised its head again. As a founder member of Sakyadhita, I was a delegate. One of the speakers scheduled was the American Buddhist, the Venerable Karma Lekshe Tsomo – one of the organizers of the 1987 conference. Her topic was to be Buddhist and Christian women's experience. Two of the Christian women who had heard Kusuma Devendra wanted to attend, just for that session. When I asked whether they could, I had a hard time gaining permission. Again, I was told by one organizer, 'You don't know how they will use it.' In the end they came. The Venerable Karma Lekshe Tsomo had no problem with them coming – after all she was going to say that some Christian nuns understood her monastic motivation better than some western Buddhists – neither did one of the Thai women organizers. And when they came, they found they knew several of the Sri Lankan *dasa sil māthās* (ten precept mothers) attending. In both these instances, the vocabulary of distorting, twisting, using, goes right back to the nineteenth century, when evangelical missionaries 'used' the hospitality of Buddhist monks for their own anti-Buddhist purposes.

In this context, a conversation with Professor Y. Karunadasa, one of the supervisors of my doctoral dissertation, is significant. No other Christian had done a doctorate at the Postgraduate Institute of Pāli and Buddhist Studies of the University of Kelaniya and no other westerner – and Professor Karunadasa was a little nervous, afraid that he could be criticized by the institution. In this conversation, he spoke of his despair about Buddhist

Christian dialogue. When he looked at Christian writing on Buddhism, he explained, some of it the product of dialogue, he saw a pattern. The writers would begin with praise and then sting, injecting poison into their accounts. He then passed to western scholarship on Buddhism. He was critical of that also, because he perceived it as concentrating on what he saw as popular Buddhism and not on Buddhist philosophy. He believed this expressed a subtle hostility to Buddhism. He, therefore, urged me to mark a new beginning and not to work against Buddhism through my doctorate. He made me realize that more hung on my doctorate than simply whether my scholarship was good enough! I would also be judged on whether I, as a Christian, could undertake a doctorate on Buddhism without a hidden agenda. The result might determine whether Christians would be welcome to do doctorates at the Institute in the future!

Sri Lanka is not the only place where inter faith dialogue continues to be conditioned by the history of colonialism and conflict. The same is true of India and, by extension, Britain. At a meeting held in the late 1990s by Churches Together in Britain and Ireland on violence against Christians in India, an invited Hindu speaker began his input by quoting the denigrating words about Hinduism of a nineteenth-century missionary. 'How would you like your faith described in this way, and would you be inclined to trust those who wrote it?' he asked. His implicit message was, 'Do not be surprised that violence breaks out against Christians in a country that has not long broken free from imperialism and still suffers great poverty.' He did not condone the violence but he could understand how it had arisen better than the Christians present. Similarly, a Christian–Hindu Forum in Britain, formed in the late 1990s, had to be disbanded in 2006–7 because of mistrust on the side of the Hindu participants. Statements by Christian organizations on caste and a report by a prominent Hindu on Christian evangelism in India were key triggers in this. It was as though the Hindu participants were still asking of Christians, 'What do you really think of Hinduism? Do you still wish to convert us to Christianity as your forefathers did? Can we trust you?' As this goes to press, there are moves towards a re-formed Christian–Hindu Forum in Britain.

The importance of a dialogue of life

Sri Lanka has taught me that a sound first step to inter faith understanding, when there is this level of mistrust between faiths, is to enable people of the faiths concerned simply to live alongside each other in a dialogue of life that has no evangelistic agenda – the second theme of the extract I quoted at the beginning of this chapter. My learning of this was supremely influenced by a visit to Alukalavita, a Buddhist village near Buttala in the Province of Uva, in the south of Sri Lanka, to stay with Father Michael Rodrigo, a Catholic priest who chose to establish a small Christian community there. I have mentioned his work before in this book, in the context of my visit to Tibbotuwawa Vihāra, and also his death. The effect he and his work had on me is inestimable and, although I have published and preached about his work before, this chapter could not be complete without him.[10]

Father Mike, as his friends called him, was born in 1927 to a Roman Catholic mother and a father of Buddhist background. At the age of 20, he joined the religious order of the Oblates of Mary Immaculate and studied theology and philosophy at the Gregorian University in Rome. It was in Rome in 1959 that he gained his first doctoral degree in Buddhist Philosophy. Between 1955 and 1971, he taught at the National Roman Catholic Seminary in Sri Lanka. During this time, he experienced a growing dissatisfaction with the theology taught there, because he believed it did not address the social and economic pressures of the time. The youth insurrection of 1971 (the first JVP insurrection), a fruit of state neglect of rural impoverishment, confirmed his views. It was in this year that he went to Paris to study for his second doctorate on the 'Moral Passover from Selfishness to Selflessness' in Christianity and the other religions of Sri Lanka.

On his return from Paris, he did not go back to the national seminary. His social consciousness had changed. In 1975, he started to work with Fr Tissa Balasuriya at The Centre for Society and Religion, a centre that was pioneering Christian engagement with human rights, poverty, unemployment and racial justice. In 1978, he moved again and became Director of Sevaka Sevana, an institute pioneering a new contextual training course for priests in the Badulla Diocese. This brought him face to face with the unwritten history of the poor of Sri Lanka and led him, in 1980, to leave his post at Sevaka Sevana for the almost entirely Buddhist village of Alukalavita. He set up Suba Seth Gedara (Good Wishes House). Two Roman Catholic sisters joined him, Milburga and Benedict. Their centre, although it eventually had a classroom and a health room, was built mainly of local materials and had no electricity or piped water. The group shared the poverty of the villagers. For in Fr Mike's words, the people were largely, at that time, 'landless, voiceless and powerless'.

The Buttala region, in the province of Uva, had been chosen not only because of the poverty of the people. Mistrust of Christianity in the area was high and Fr Mike traced it back to the Uva Rebellion against the 'Christian' British of 1818, which had been crushed using brutal force, including the scorching of agricultural land, the destruction of 'tanks' in the area (artificial lakes, masterpieces of ancient engineering, used for irrigation and domestic purposes) and the killing of young people over 18. The memory of this had not died, Fr Mike was convinced, and the horror of it was linked with Christianity. Fr Mike's aim was to create trust where there was mistrust. He did not, there-fore, build a church – that would have split the village in two. He simply created a Christian presence that was supportive of the Buddhist ethos of the village. Nevertheless, at first, there was intense mistrust of the new community. One Buddhist monk made it clear that the people wanted him to go, fearing that his aim was proselytization. What they found was very different.

The villagers found that Fr Mike and the sisters joined with Buddhists in their religious celebrations, and that they were willing to work with the people to defend their rights, for instance against sugar multinationals that were taking over land in the region. In 1981, at Vesak, Fr Mike stood up in one of the local *vihāras* and praised the Five Buddhist Precepts. When 89 farmers lost their harvest due to drought, he prepared a 34-page report and travelled with Buddhist monks and farmers to gain redress and relief at the local state office. For Vesak in 1982, he worked with the Buddhist lyricist in the village to write some devotional songs based on the ten Buddhist 'perfections': generosity, morality, renunciation, wisdom, energy, patience, effort, concentration and wisdom. By that point, mistrust had evaporated. After those songs had been sung, the Buddhist monk who had originally asked him to leave announced that he was happy for the people to go both to the Buddhist *vihāra* and Suba Seth Gedara.

Fr Mike did not think he was in any way compromising his Christian faith. On the contrary, he believed that he was witnessing to the true heart of Christianity, which should affirm goodness wherever it is found. When I was at Suba Seth Gedara, never did he stress what divided Buddhism and Christianity but only what united them – qualities such as loving kindness, compassion, sharing, rejection of greed, renunciation and patience. So, when relating to Buddhists, he always stressed these qualities. He also claimed he had re-learnt them 'at the feet of the people'. To affirm all this was not, he felt, in contradiction with his Christian beliefs.

Central to his awareness was that people from different religions needed to work together, to co-operate rather than compete. His was a dialogue of presence moving to a dialogue of life and then to dialogues of religious experience and social action. His view was that it was only through these forms of dialogue that

Jesus could be confessed in a Buddhist context and only through a radical identification with the poor. And he justified this by pointing to the way in which attitudes to Christianity changed during his time in the village in Uva. He quoted frequently the words of a youth leader, several years after Suba Seth Gedara had been established:

I accept Jesus as the founder of a noble religion, one who showed sincere affection for the people. He loved all as equals and showed it by his life . . .

At the start, some young people watched you carefully. 'How will you act towards us? Did you come to turn us to your ways somehow? Were you an international spy-group or spy-ring to eventually sell out our village?' were the questions harassing us youth. But we went beyond observation, worked with you as you worked with the people. There we discovered the true face of what you called *sabhava*, the church . . .

If anyone asked me, I would say: 'we know them as Christians' by the name of Jesus they possess and profess . . . The villagers cannot be torn apart from this group . . . [11]

If Fr Mike had entered with the usual Christian agenda – to establish a church – the results would not have been the same. Division and bitterness would have been caused and those who remained Buddhist would have had a negative interpretation of Christianity confirmed. Simply being with the people, standing with them in distress, documenting injustices against them, meant that Buddhists could glimpse that compassion and self-giving love lay at the heart of the Christian concept of God.

When I visited Alukalavita, the centre was well established. I arrived tired and dusty, the government bus from Colombo having had a puncture, lengthening the journey from eight to ten hours. I slept on a wooden bench covered with a thin piece of foam and a mat, and washed at the well, protected from view by corrugated iron sheeting. The centre was packed with resources – a garden of herbal remedies; a cupboard filled with films and slide shows on such things as Cuba, tea, the environment, culture – even a filmstrip on Scrooge with Sinhala soundtrack, shown at Christmas. During my time there, I was taken to visit the two Buddhist *vihāras* that Fr Mike worked with. I have already spoken about the second, Tibbotuwawa Vihāra. The first was to meet Ven. Alutwela Sumanasiri. When we arrived, he was sleeping off the effects of three all-night Pirit sessions. That he came out at all was a testimony to his relationship with Fr Mike. I raised many questions: What opportunities for meditation do you give the people? What aspects of *dhamma* do you stress in your sermons? What teaching do you give young people? How to live a better life on a personal plane in harmony with the *brahmavihāras* (loving kindness, compassion, sympathetic joy and equanimity) was his main message when preaching. Meditation he left to specialist centres. 'We are a poor region and temple,' he stressed. As we talked, village boys joined us and sat on the floor in a relaxed, informal way, completely at home with the *bhikkhu*.[12]

The visit had a profound effect on me. Let me quote from my diary of the time:

I have so many memories of my time near Buttala. To bathe at the well as dusk became night and the air tinged with coolness was delicious. As we went around the village one day, coconuts were chopped down for us, freshly picked sweetcorn cooked and wood apples pressed into our hands. Although poor, people gave spontaneously and joyfully. I also remember the refectory and watching the sun dancing on the mud walls as we ate red rice and vegetables, while the cats searched for our laps.

Then there was the daily Mass at evening. Shirani (a young trainee at the centre), Sister Benedict (Sr Milburga was away),

Father Michael and myself would sit in dim lamplight. The petromax lamp needed a new mantle so, instead of brightness, we were surrounded by a Rembrandt-like glow. The bread and wine took on a new significance in the quiet darkness. It was an act offered up for the blessing of the whole village, a lifting up of the people to God. Sister Benedict, with her long plait falling over her shoulder, Father Mike with his orange stole, Shirani sitting by the wall and myself were united in something beyond words. The Mass was a living core from which strength flowed into us and then outwards into the village. Stripped of gilt and gold, it became a Mass of the poor, a Mass of unlimited strength.[13]

It was when saying Mass that Fr Mike was shot in the head, at point blank range, later that year on 10 November 1987. His brains were spattered on the women participating, Shirani, Benedict and Milburga. His killers have never been found but they were certainly not of the village. Perhaps it was his opposition to the sugar multinationals that was the cause or his insistence that the JVP should not use violence to gain their ends. I had been due to visit him again at the end of the month.

Both his life and his death have taught me more than I can say. In Sri Lanka and Britain, if people of other faiths are to come to a deeper understanding of what Christianity is, in contexts where there is mistrust because Christianity has been linked with imperial power, then they must see a non-threatening Christianity in action. This is what the villagers of Alukalavita saw. This is what changed their perceptions utterly.

I found this dialogue of life at several other centres in Sri Lanka, some with charismatic Christian leaders who are now ageing. I do not think that the Buddhists of Alukalavita ever shared Mass with Fr Mike. That would have been a step too far. At Satyodaya, a centre I mentioned in the last chapter, however, Buddhists and Hindus did attend a Mass, on Christmas Eve, at midnight. I was invited there on my very first Christmas in Sri Lanka. Satyodaya, in Kandy, was founded by Paul Casperz SJ to be a centre for research on and work in the plantations of the central hill country. When I was visiting it, a community of Sinhala, Tamil and Burgher (Paul Casperz was a Burgher, descended from the Portuguese or Dutch), Buddhist, Christian and Hindu, worked there.

In preparation for the Mass, the common room of the centre was cleared of its chairs. Mats and cushions replaced them, facing a low, white-covered table, on which stood two slender vases of flowers, a candle and liturgical books. By midnight, the room was full of adults and children. Fr Paul dressed in spotless white entered and sat cross-legged on a white, raised cushion behind the table, followed by his elderly dog and Roshan, a young boy who would help him throughout the Mass. The Mass, in Sinhala, was beautiful, lyrical, with no western carols. Just 12 received the elements, including two or three children. It was only then that I realized that the others were either Buddhist or Hindu, mainly Buddhist from a nearby village that Satyodaya worked in. After the Mass, bananas, cakes and biscuits were shared. Goodwill flowed. By 1.00 a.m. a few of the younger ones lay sleeping; others seemed ready to stay awake all night. The stars were brilliant and the breeze tossed balloons away from the clutching fingers of the children.[14]

That Christmas Mass was not a threat to the Buddhists and Hindus who attended. Fr Paul was simply their priest and Satyodaya their centre. They could be themselves. They could celebrate Christmas with joy and partake of the food that followed, knowing there was no pressure on them to convert.

A similar ethos has moulded the activities of Devasarana Development Centre near Kurunegala, which I have mentioned in connection with the 1989 Martyrs' Day. It was founded in 1957 as Devasaranamaya, a vegetarian Christian religious community inspired by Indian Christian ashrams that sought harmony with the religious traditions of India. The regime was strict, with its members committed to celibacy, poverty and obedience, under its founder Revd Yohan Devananda. Its aim was to create a praying, witnessing community that lived close to the people of the nearby village. When I visited it, in the 1980s, silence and prayer played a much less important part. It had become a multi-faith community, including Buddhists, Christians, Hindus and Marxists, that was engaging with issues such as land reform, unemployment and the status of women. The change had come because the ashram members had been challenged by the villagers to greater involvement. It still exists in 2009. Important for the concern of this book is that by the 1970s it had developed a liturgy that people of all religions could use – A New World Liturgy, which included readings from the Upanishads, the Christian Gospels, the Buddhist Suttas, the Qur'an, Marx and Mao Tse Tung. Some of its words seem dated now but it was pioneering in its time, and sought to open up a 'living dialogue'. Its founder, Yohan Devananda, is still active in national peace and reconciliation issues.

I cannot leave this topic without mentioning a couple of the women who, in a less visible way, have worked tirelessly for an interreligious dialogue of life. Audrey Rebera is one. Now in her seventies, she was instrumental in forming 'Mothers and Daughters of Lanka', an inter faith women's organization. It was working at the height of the unrest between 1988 and 1993, bringing Buddhist, Christian, Hindu and Muslim women together, and was a sign of hope for many. Unfortunately, it is no longer in existence but the solidarity it expressed is now present in other women's organizations. Other twentieth-century pioneers of a women's dialogue of life include Malini Devananda, Pearl Stephen, Pauline Hensman, Annathaie Abeyesekera and Ann Abayasekera.

Challenging misrepresentations

To the two themes mentioned at the beginning of this chapter I have since added many more. These are related to a dialogue of life but also go beyond it. They include how misconceptions can be challenged, how difference between religions should be dealt with and the enrichment that can flow from moving into or having deep dialogue with another religious world view.

In Sri Lanka, I found it disturbing but salutary to listen both to the misconceptions about Christianity that some Buddhists held and to the serious problems with Christianity that some who knew Christianity well voiced to me. For instance, a few weeks before I left Sri Lanka after completing my doctorate and after seven years of study of Buddhism, I was at a lunch party and fell into conversation with a young Buddhist woman. After hearing that I was a Christian and had studied Buddhism for over seven years, she expressed amazement that I had not converted and added something like this, 'But you only have a lesser goal, you only worship a god. You don't have *nibbāna*.' I could see where she was coming from. In Sri Lankan Buddhism, there are gods but they are in need of the Buddha's teaching, for the heavens in which they reside are within the round of birth and rebirth. The Buddha is described in the Pāli Canon as 'teacher of gods and humans'. These gods can be petitioned for mundane blessings but they have nothing to do with gaining ultimate liberation. Many Buddhists in Sri Lanka assume that Christianity is only about the worship of one of these gods. If they do think beyond this, the image they often have of the Christian god is of an inscrutable external force, who metes out punishment and joy arbitrarily, leading to fatalism in devotees. Buddhists in Sri Lanka also express surprise when told that Christians sometimes meditate or sit in silent contemplation.

Then, there was Professor Lily de Silva, who once shared with me that Christianity had always seemed 'thin' to her because it did not set down a path to liberation. Moreover, it seemed to encourage people to escape personal responsibility by placing everything at the feet of God. 'Christians in church just seem to praise and expect God's grace to do it all!' she declared. Set against her knowledge of the Pāli texts, this, frankly, seemed ridiculous.

Inter faith dialogue must be able to tease out misconceptions about Christianity and to challenge them. Not all the perceptions about Christianity that Buddhists voiced to me, however, were misconceptions. Some were criticisms. That Christians believe living beings only have one life to 'get it right' can strike Buddhists as cruel and almost inconceivable. Inconceivable also in its cruelty is the fact that some Christians believe that hell is eternal. In Buddhism a sojourn in one of the hells is temporary. A hell dweller may, in her next life, find herself in a heaven or a human being on earth.

Then, certain aspects of Jesus' ministry can cause problems. I can remember a conversation about Jesus with another close Buddhist friend, the American *bhikkhunī*, the Venerable Miao Kwang Sudharma. There was something that had always puzzled her about Jesus, she explained. How could someone who breathed compassion and calm suddenly lose control in the temple and overturn the tables of the money changers like an angry maniac? For her, Jesus was a *bodhisattva*, a Buddha-to-be, who, in the giving of his life to save others, was mastering the 'perfection' of generosity. But his anger in the temple courtyard in Jerusalem made her question this. She remembered passion plays when the contrast leapt out and caused confusion. Could an evolved person act like that? In Buddhism, anger is always negative. It draws one away from seeing the world with equanimity and compassion. Her puzzlement was genuine. The idea that there could be an anger that was positive simply did not resonate with her.

These were just a few of the misconceptions and criticisms of Christianity that Buddhists voiced to me, because there was trust between us. If trust had not been built, they would not have been voiced. I would suggest that Christians need to hear how their religion can appear to other people of faith and to bear in mind that not all the criticisms voiced will be misconceptions. Some will point to the very real differences between religious world views and it is here that listening rather than defensiveness is necessary.

Where faiths touch

If I mentioned only the criticisms, however, I would be doing an injustice to the range of conversations I have had about Christianity with Buddhists. I remember particularly my conversations with Sr Nyanasiri. When we first started to talk, she often challenged me about how I could be drawn to Buddhism and yet remain a Christian. 'What about the concepts of rebirth, *kamma* or the lack of a creator God in Buddhism? Can you accept these?' she would say with just a touch of humour. As our friendship grew, however, we spoke more of meditation and mysticism. She had read Evelyn Underhill's book, *Mysticism*[15] and had come to believe that there was a graduated mystical path that was the same for people of all religions, although they might use different terms to express it. Where Underhill spoke of recollection, she pointed out, Buddhists might speak of concentration or one-pointedness. And all religions spoke of the naughting of the self in meditation and contemplation. So surely, she would speculate, there must be a point where different frameworks become irrelevant. She also told me of a conversation she had had with the Venerable Nyanaponika (1901–94), the German convert to Buddhism, resident for most of his life in Sri Lanka, for whom Sr Nyanasiri did much administrative work. They had been speaking about the lack of descriptive material about the *jhānas* (meditative absorptions) in Buddhist literature. The Venerable Nyanaponika had told her that he believed the best description of them came in the writings of St John of the Cross.

An experiment in dialogue through art

At Tulana Research Centre I encountered another level of this kind of encounter – Buddhists 'evangelizing' Christians through art, not the evangelism that would seek to convert Christians to Buddhism but that which teaches Christians what Christianity truly is. Tulana is a constant in my journey. I have mentioned more than once the help that its Director, Aloysius Pieris (b. 1934), gave me in my early years and the work I did at Tulana as his Research Assistant. Pieris joined the Jesuit Order as a young man and was asked to concentrate on Indological research, although his first loves were music and maths. As Rodrigo, he has a double doctorate – one in Buddhism, one in Christian theology. He was the first Christian, let alone priest, to obtain a PhD in Buddhism at a Sri Lankan University in the early 1970s. He is fluent in Pāli, Sanskrit, Latin and several modern European languages and is both an Indologist and a Christian liberation theologian. Tulana Research Centre was conceived in the early 1970s and founded in 1974 as a new experiment in dialogue, hospitality, community, research and awareness raising. The name itself means discernment, weighing up, discerning action. In 1982, it moved into its present buildings.

This is how I first described the centre in 1986:

Tulana Research Centre, situated about eight miles from Colombo, at Kelaniya, is an aesthetic jewel ... Its roofs, its mellow walls and its contours remind me of a temple ... There is an appreciation of beauty down to the last detail. Leaves and petals are sketched into the stone of the pathways between the library and meditation room ... To cross into the library, one steps across a rainwater pool, placing one's foot on a circular stone, which hints of a lotus. I have never been to a garden or temple influenced by Zen but Tulana may speak the same language.[16]

Many more buildings have now been added. There are now, in 2009, three libraries with plans for a completely new library building to house the Centre's ever-growing collection of Sinhala, English and antiquarian books. The Centre now has five programmes: Research and Encounter; Social Animation; the Media Unit; the Peace Desk; the Centre for Education of Hearing-impaired Children. Inter faith encounter through art is part of the first. When I first visited Tulana, there were two pieces of art in the main community room, one on a Christian theme and one on a Buddhist theme, both done by a Buddhist monk, the Venerable Hattigammana Uttarananda. The largest was a frieze of Christ washing the feet of his disciples. The setting, though, was Asian. The disciples wore the robes of Asian renunciants and carried their black alms bowls, and Jesus was the master of the house they were entering, stooping to wash their feet. The other showed the Buddha sending out his monks to preach the *dhamma*, one by one.

Now there are many more pieces of art: the Pieta described in Chapter 1; the mural of Christ in the temple at Jerusalem mentioned in the Introduction; the four sites that caused the Buddha to renounce his life of luxury; Jesus receiving water from a woman at a well in Samaria; a woman playing a stringed instrument who is both Sarasvati and Mary, Mother of God. Generally speaking all the works on Christian themes are by Buddhist artists and all the ones on Buddhist themes are by Christians. This embodies one of Tulana's key aspirations – not towards syncretism or synthesis between religions but symbiosis, through which, 'Each religion, challenged by the other religion's unique approach to the liberationist aspiration of the poor . . . discovers and renames itself in its specificity in response to other approaches'.[17]

It is an approach through which Buddhists can help Christians 'see' what they may have forgotten within Christianity and vice versa. Pieris will say to visitors to Tulana, 'We ask Buddhists to tell us who Christ is.' But it is not any Buddhist. Only those who are also engaged in working for the good of the people who, in Pieris's words, are in touch with the 'Unspoken speaker', have the spiritual authority to do this.

The Buddhist monk, the Venerable Hattigammana Uttarananda, when he entered into dialogue in preparation for the mural of Christ washing the feet of the disciples, was, according to Pieris, already involved in campaigns for ethnic justice in the island. Pieris described the process in this way:

He spent a few months reading the scriptures and studying my collection of Christian art with the intention of holding an exhibition of paintings on Christ and the Buddha. The suggestion was that the artist does not duplicate in his Christian paintings what is already found in Buddhism. What is unique in Christianity was the object of the search. It was finally decided that the picture he would do for me was of Jesus washing the feet of the disciples (John 13.1–17). Here, in a lifesize cement embossment the artist brings out Jesus as the voluntary Slave of his sisters and brothers . . .

Thus something that has also appeared *unique* about Christ has been discovered for us by this monk: that Jesus makes sense in Asia only when he scandalizes the feudal society by manifesting himself as the one who becomes the slave of the slaves of this earth. Since then my reading of Philippians 2.6–11 has not been the same.[18]

Uttarananda, in his choosing of Jesus washing the feet of his disciples, was, according to Pieris, 'evangelizing' Christians, uncovering what is so often forgotten in a rich church.

Taking difference seriously: creativity and complementarity

The process through which the art at Tulana has evolved takes difference seriously. It affirms that Buddhism and Christianity are not the same, that each arose in a different milieu and that each has a different motif at its heart.[19] It is from their differences, however, that they give to each other, as Buddhists interpret what they see in Christianity for Christians, and vice versa. Difference is not threat but promise, and not for competition but for creativity and mutual enrichment. Differences become complementary and reciprocal as Buddhists and Christians seek to make sense of both *dukkha*, and liberation or salvation. Difference leads to symbiosis between religions.

How difference should be accommodated is one of the most challenging questions for anyone involved in inter faith relations. Some approaches seek to minimize difference, stressing only commonality, in the conviction that this will help people of different faiths to work together. The result, though, can be hurtful to some. Professor Karundasa once said to me, with evident consternation, 'Why is it that at every inter faith gathering I attend, people assume that God is the thing that unites us all. It's not God. It's humanity!' Some Buddhists are not overly worried by God language and, in inter-faith meetings, will try to translate it into a concept that is more Buddhist; others feel completely overlooked, because their identity has not been recognized. I could sympathize with Karunadasa. Members of theistic religions should not make the mistake of believing that all religions are like them and place God at the centre. Neither, though, should they see this difference as an unbridgeable barrier between themselves and Buddhism.

Other approaches to inter faith relations elevate difference by claiming that inter faith dialogue must involve measuring difference and debating truth claims to see which are most reasonable.

The middle way between the two, the one that I favour, is to recognize that faiths touch and diverge. The differences between faiths are as real as the touching points and should not be pushed under the carpet. For to respect difference is to respect the integrity of another faith. It is to avoid the domination that Hema Gunatileke talked about.

Some differences between faiths are difficult to reconcile with each other and call simply for recognition. Some can be reconciled through conversation. Others offer radical challenges to Christians when engaged with creatively, opening the doors to change and enrichment. Let me give two examples of the latter. Kenneth Fernando, Director of the Ecumenical Institute for Study and Dialogue, later Bishop of Colombo, once said to me:

The strongest point about Christianity is that there is a Saviour. The strongest point about Buddhism is that there is no Saviour.[20]

The difference between Buddhism and Christianity that Fernando was highlighting would seem to be stark, the emphasis in Buddhism on self-effort and in Christianity on the external action of a Saviour. But the way the comparison is phrased invites Christians to interrogate themselves rather than assume superiority, by asking: Can the concept of a Saviour be abused? Can Christians forget that Jesus invited all his followers to a challenging, self-sacrificial way of life, by placing too much emphasis on the saving action of Christ? Does Christianity need a corrective from Buddhism here, one that might address Lily de Silva's misconception that Christianity is 'thin'? I am not sure whether Fernando would answer yes to all these questions but I would. Fernando's masterly sentence encapsulates what I mean by difference between religions bearing creative potential within it.

The second example is my own struggle with the concept of *anattā*, non-self, which can seem to diverge dramatically from the Christian concept of a soul. However, I have come to see that Christianity and Buddhism are not as far away from each other, on the question of the self, as could at first be thought.

The concept of *anattā* was originally taught by the Buddha in a context where other religious groups were beginning to speak of an unchanging essence within the human person that was the same as the godhead. It was this that the Buddha disagreed with. The mind and body just does not work like that, he stressed. Everything within them is impermanent, ever changing and interdependent. It is impossible to extract something from them and call it a soul or self. He certainly did not deny that we were persons or that there was continuity after death through a chain of cause and effect, only the possibility of an unchanging self. What might have begun as a statement about how our bodies and minds worked, then came to function within the tradition as a doctrine to aid the letting go of 'me', 'mine' and 'I' – the selfishness that leads us away from *nibbāna*. As one of the members of the small women's group with which I shared my first Vesak once said to me, 'If there is no belief in self, there is no worry, only a sense of release. If there is no self, there is no reason to become angry or hurt. Competition between people is unnecessary. Fear is taken away.' In other words, the doctrine came to be linked with liberation.

As I have written in another autobiographical piece, reflection on this soon brought Bible passages and Christian liturgy to mind. For instance, I thought of Paul's statement, 'For you have died and your life is hid with Christ in God' (Colossians 3.3) and the sentence said by all Methodists in January at the annual Covenant Service, 'I am no longer my own but thine. Put me to what thou wilt . . .'. Both seemed to resonate with the heart of the *anattā* doctrine in their message that the self has to be given up.[21] Difference was present between the two, certainly. In Christianity, one forgets the self to offer oneself to God. In Buddhism, there is no personal higher power of this kind. Yet, as I wrote in 2000:

Both Christianity and Buddhism point to the liberation that can come when any wish to protect the self is transcended. Buddhism goes further than Christianity, by saying that the whole idea of an unchanging soul is false. But, paradoxically, the very fact that Buddhism goes further has made me see the gospel message in a more radical light. I have become uncomfortable with the Christian piety that plays into western individualism by stressing individual salvation; this feeds the self's sense of security and avoids the demand for self-renunciation.[22]

I might have phrased this slightly differently if I had drawn on the excellent comparative study of *anattā* and soul by Sri Lankan Methodist minister, Lynn de Silva, in which he contests that Judaism and the early Christian tradition believed in an unchanging soul. It is a masterly exploration that demonstrates that the two religions touch at a profound level in their theories of self.[23] The process that brought me also to this conclusion was one that began with taking difference seriously and then progressed, through reflection and the willingness to be challenged, to a point where I could see that there were far more touching points than I had thought, touching points that could challenge each faith.

The following words, written in an introduction to a book I co-edited with a western Buddhist, Ramona Kauth, explain further what I am trying to say about the creativity of difference:

My own belief is that the encounter between Buddhists and Christians is one of the most significant inter-religious meetings of our time, not only because of the touching points between the two religions but because of the challenges Buddhists and Christians can give to each other through difference. Every meeting between a Christian and a Buddhist is potentially dynamic, enriching and life-enhancing. Ramona and I, for instance, in editing this book, spent many tremendously exciting hours simply talking about Buddhism. It is an experience I shall always be thankful for. The dynamism in such encounters, I hope, will not only touch metaphysics but also the whole area of practice and discipleship, to use a Buddhist and a Christian term. Both Buddhism and Christianity emphasize action. The two religions may have most to give to one another at the point when questions such as the following are asked: What does activist compassion mean? How can we train our minds for effective, discerning action in the world? How can a peaceful, just society be worked towards? [24]

As I hope this chapter has shown, my journey into Buddhism has formed my attitude to inter faith encounter in more ways than I expressed at the end of my first year in Sri Lanka. My awareness that inter faith encounter always takes place in a context conditioned by history, politics and power relationships remains, as does my conviction that a dialogue of life can help to redress mistrust. Added to these is excitement about what faiths can give to each other, although seeing oneself through the eyes of 'the other' can be painful. I remain committed to the need to respect differences between faiths but see them as opportunities for creativity rather than threat. For me the goal of all of this must be insight into the meaning of existence and into how a better world can be worked towards.

Notes

1 See Elizabeth J. Harris, 2006, *Theravāda Buddhism and the British Encounter: Religious, Missionary and Colonial Experience in Nineteenth-Century Sri Lanka*, Abingdon and New York: Routledge.

2 See Richard F. Young and G. S. B. Senanayake, 1998, *The Carpenter Heretic: A Collection of Buddhist Stories about Christianity from Eighteenth-Century Sri Lanka*, Colombo: Karunaratne & Sons, which is a translation of folk stories from the Dutch colonial period in Sri

Lanka that ridicule Jesus. Mentioned in Harris, 2006, *Theravāda Buddhism and the British Encounter*, p. 192.

3 See Harris, 2006, *Theravāda Buddhism and the British Encounter*, p. 192.

4 Robert Spence Hardy, 1865, *The Jubilee Memorials of the Wesleyan Mission, South Ceylon*, Colombo: Wesleyan Mission Press, p. 286, quoted in Harris, 2006, *Theravāda Buddhism and the British Encounter*, p. 193.

5 Harris, 2006, *Theravāda Buddhism and the British Encounter*, p. 198.

6 Harris, 2006, *Theravāda Buddhism and the British Encounter*, p. 195.

7 T. Moscrop, 1894, 'Christianity and Buddhism in South Ceylon: a missionary speech' in *Monthly Literary Register* (Colombo), II, New Series 12, December 1894, pp. 285–7. Quoted in Harris, 2006, *Theravāda Buddhism and the British Encounter*, p. 201.

8 See Harris, 2006, *Theravāda Buddhism and the British Encounter*, p. 202 where I draw on a transcription of the debate by J. M. Peebles.

9 C. W. Leadbeater, 'Wesak/Wesak Compliments' in *The Buddhist*, I, 22, pp. 172–4, here pp. 173–4, quoted in Harris, 2006, *Theravāda Buddhism and the British Encounter*, p. 204.

10 See for instance, Elizabeth J. Harris, 2000, 'Competition, Cooperation and Reconciliation in Inter-Faith Relations: Part two of a series on Evangelism and Dialogue' in the *Thinking Mission* series, London: USPG.

11 Michael Rodrigo, 'Buddhism and Christianity: Towards a Human Future: An Example of a Village Dialogue of Life', in *Fr Mike and his Thought*, vol. 2, Logos, vol. 27, no. 4, October 1988, Colombo: Centre for Society and Religion, p. 25, reworked as Michael Rodrigo, 'The Hope of Liberation Lessens Man's Inhumanity: A Contribution to Dialogue at Village Level' in R. S. Sugirtharajah (ed.), 1993, *Asian Faces of Jesus*, London: SCM Press, pp. 189–210. See also Harris, 2000, *Competition, Co-operation and Reconciliation in Inter-Faith Relations*, p. 7.

12 Based on unpublished diary, 5 January 1987.

13 Unpublished diary, 7 January 1987.

14 Adapted from unpublished diary entries for December 1986.

15 Evelyn Underhill, first published 1911, *Mysticism: The Development of Humankind's Spiritual Consciousness*, London: Methuen & Co.

16 Unpublished diary for 10 August 1986.

17 Aloysius Pieris, 1996, *Fire and Water: Basic Issues in Asian Buddhism and Christianity*, Maryknoll, NY: Orbis, p. 161.

18 Pieris, 1996, 'Inculturation in Asia: A Theological Reflection on Experience' in Pieris, *Fire and Water*, pp. 133–4.

19 See Aloysius Pieris, 1988, 'Christianity in a Core to Core Dialogue with Buddhism' in *Love Meets Wisdom: A Christian Experience of Buddhism*, Maryknoll, NY: Orbis, pp. 110–35, in which Pieris speaks of Buddhism as having an idiom of gnosis and Christianity, of agape. He claims that an obstacle to Christian–Buddhist understanding has been a failure to acknowledge the reciprocity between the two idioms.

20 Unpublished diary, 10 February 1987.

21 See Harris, 2000, 'The Beginning of Something being Broken', pp. 15–16.

22 Harris, 2000, 'The Beginning of Something Being Broken', p. 16.

23 Lynn de Silva, 1975, *The Problem of the Self in Buddhism and Christianity*, Colombo: The Study Centre for Religion and Society (Now the Ecumenical Institute for Study and Dialogue).

24 Ramona Kauth and Elizabeth J. Harris (eds), 2004, *Meeting Buddhists*, Leicester: Christians Aware, p. 13.

Epilogue

My journey has given me riches for which I am enormously grateful: a new language of the spirit, a new way of seeing the world. But I can offer no reassuring platitudes about being strengthened in my own faith through my encounter with Buddhism. Neither can I say that the journey has turned me towards the riches in my own tradition, and brought me to appreciate these more deeply. These often repeated claims I find too comfortable. My 'passing over and coming back' has been somehow different.[1]

I wrote this in 2000 about my journey into a faith not my own. I would say the same now, although not quite so bluntly, since the riches of my own tradition still hold me strongly in their grasp. My journey was not orientated towards being strengthened in my own faith. It was about entering another religious world view and speaking another religious 'language', because such other 'languages' exist and spiritually feed millions of people. The journey contained desert experiences as I let go in order to 'pass over' but the overall experience was marked by growth and incredible enrichment. It was about going where I did not know, changing and arriving back at a different place. It was about discovering differences, convergences and complementarities that made me interrogate what I believed and how I believed it. Now, when I deal with everyday problems, answers that draw on Buddhism will come to my mind just as speedily as Christian ones. Sometimes, they arrive first! But I am not a Buddhist-Christian. I remain a Christian, but one who draws deeply from the wisdom of another faith as well.

This book opens a window on the differences, convergences and complementarities I discovered. It does this by implication rather than prescription. A compare and contrast method would not have allowed Buddhism to arise with an integrity of its own and it would not have been true to my Buddhist friends. Yet, each chapter, except the first, contains at least one main thought or practice that I believe non-Buddhists can learn from. Let me mention these now.

Chapter 2 looked at the human condition from a Buddhist perspective and stressed the importance, in Buddhist analysis, of *dukkha*, and greed or craving. It argued that this results in a realistic appraisal of the forces at work in the world. This view does not deny that human existence contains goodness, compassion and joy. But it emphasizes what humans can do to beauty through their greed. It is a message, I would suggest, that Christians need to hear. Church services can glide over this through an outdated, complacent and superficial stress on the beauty of the world. A hymn such as 'All things bright and beautiful' has stuck in my throat numerous times because it seems to speak of a different world from the one most of us inhabit, especially where there is war, human rights abuses and poverty. It is not, however, a message that is alien to the Christian tradition. As Fr Mike pointed out to me, Psalm 90 can be seen as a hymn to *dukkha*:

> You tell man to return to what he was;
> you change him back to dust.
> A thousand years to you are like one day;
> they are like yesterday, already gone,
> like a short hour in the night.
> You carry us away like a flood;
> we last no longer than a dream.
> We are like weeds that sprout in the morning,

that grow and burst into bloom,
then dry up and die in the evening.

Chapter 3 stressed that Buddhism and Christianity touch in their vision of what lies at the heart of the cosmos: compassion and wisdom for Buddhists; self-giving love for Christians. It also suggested, however, that Buddhism can help Christians remember that detachment, or non-attachment as I would prefer to call it, and compassionate action are interdependent, each necessary if the other is to be truly effective.

In Chapter 4, I reflected on the fact that the aspect of Buddhism I was initially most wary of, *vipassanā* meditation, was the one that, in the end, taught me most. It is a principle that I would suggest could be extended to other inter faith encounters. Bare attention or mindfulness has become part of my spiritual practice. I need it and I believe most people would benefit from some form of this practice. It is not, however, absent from Christianity. The hesychastic tradition in particular touches Buddhist practice here. Mystics in all religious traditions have long known that, to avoid burn-out, we must be still.

Chapter 5 touched on what Buddhism can teach us about the understanding and transforming of violence, one of the most intractable problems in our world. In its realism, its emphasis on cause and conditioning, and its insights into how the mind constructs its own realities from faulty premises, Buddhism can offer us much, not least an admission that violent tendencies are hard to eradicate.

Chapter 6 sought to convey insights from my Sri Lankan teachers that can help the inter faith task wherever it is undertaken. It stressed what many inter faith practitioners discover – that their encounters with people of other faiths are conditioned by history and power relationships. It gave examples of the changes that could come from a dialogue of life but also stressed what can come after this, in terms of honest, respectful conversation, mutual enrichment and what Pieris has called, symbiosis. Here, I would suggest, the West has much to learn from what is happening in countries such as Sri Lanka.

What theology do I draw on to be able to advise such interreligious learning? I have often been asked this question by Christians who believe the entire message of the Bible is contained in verses such as John 14.6 (Jesus answered him, 'I am the way, the truth and the life; no one goes to the Father, except by me.'). Fr Michael Rodrigo once said to me as we talked in Suba Seth Gedara, 'I could not be a Christian, if the God Christians worshipped condemned non-Christians.' Wesley Ariarajah, a Sri Lankan Methodist minister, who worked on the inter faith desk of the World Council of Churches for many years, made a similar point at the beginning of his book, *Not Without My Neighbour*. As a child, he lived in an almost entirely Hindu village in the north of Sri Lanka. Hindu friends would join his family for prayer, and he would join in Hindu prayers. When, as a young adult, he was told, by Christian evangelists, that his devout, ethically conscientious Hindu neighbours would go to hell, he was uncomfortable, feeling it would be 'unfair on the part of God to receive us, the Christian family, into heaven and send our next-door Hindu neighbours to hell'.[2] He later found himself thinking about those people who, having been involved in inter faith encounter, would not want to be in a 'heaven' to which their neighbours would be denied. I am sure he included himself among them.

I also could not worship a God who was jealously exclusive and I am convinced the Bible does not ask this of me. Verses such as John 14.6 can be interpreted in less than exclusive ways and, certainly, should not be forced to carry the whole message of the Bible. This means that I would not dream of attempting to convert my Buddhist friends to Christianity. That would make an absolute mockery of having learnt at their feet and would be to repeat what Buddhists experienced in the nineteenth century. Most important, I am convinced that there is no biblical imperative for me to do anything of the kind. I am convinced that the God of the Bible affirms goodness, compassion, self-sacrifice, non-violence, greedlessness wherever it is found. In Christian terminology, these are the signs of a people who are close to what Christians call the kingdom of God. There is not time for me to go into the theology of this in great depth but others have done so. I would particularly recommend Kenneth Cracknell's work.[3]

In my time as Secretary for Inter Faith Relations for the Methodist Church, I sought to convey some of these insights as well as help people struggle with verses such as John 14.6 and Acts 4.12. I encouraged people to see them against the background of the whole Bible and of Jesus' example in relating to the non-Jewish 'other'. The last formal presentation I gave in this role was at an ecumenical study day in the St Albans Diocese. In it I quoted the words of John Wesley, who was able to declare, when speaking of those who are not Christian:

> Let it be observed, I purposely add, 'to those that are under the Christian dispensation', because I have no authority from the word of God 'to judge those that are without'. Nor do I conceive any man living has a right to sentence all the heathen and Mahometan world to damnation. It is far better to leave them to him that made them, and who is 'the Father of the spirits of all flesh': who is the God of the heathens as well as Christians, and who hateth nothing that he has made.
>
> (John Wesley in Sermon 130, *On living without God*)

I ended my presentation in this way:

> I believe we have lost time and energy in our Christian mission to create a better world because we have not seen people of other faiths as potential allies. We have lost chances for gaining greater insight and wisdom by not seeing interaction with people of other faiths as necessary for our own wholeness. In

other words we have lost out because we have not seen the religious resources of the world as resources that can help us.

I began with two stories (these were two cameos of inter faith relations in Britain). Let me end with two quotations:

Dialogical communion with the other is possible only when I recognize the partner as a possible source for my truth and salvation, or at least my understanding of my truth and salvation.

When I look for spiritual community, I need to find it in a wider context than simply the Buddhist community.

The first was said by a Christian, Michael von Brück. He was speaking at a conference in Sweden on 'What do I expect Buddhists to find in Jesus?' The second came from a Zen Buddhist nun, who was working in Cambodia among the poor. It was said at a Buddhist women's conference in Cambodia during a session on inter faith dialogue. I continued:

Taken together, they present two challenges: to recognize the person of another faith as a source of our salvation and truth; to create spiritual communities that are not restricted to one faith but that draw together people of different faiths. I would offer both of these challenges to you today. If we can affirm that the Word of God is wider than the Christian Church, or that God's mission extends beyond it, then we should also be able to see the need to gain insights from our neighbours of other faiths, recognising that we may not agree with all that they share with us. So, in closing, I would suggest that being Christian in a multi faith society involves mutuality, respect and sharing between faiths at the levels of doctrine, faith, spirituality and action.[4]

This is a fitting way to end this book too.

Notes

1 Harris, 2002, *The Beginning of Something Being Broken*, p. 14.

2 S. Wesley Ariarajah, 1999, *Not Without My Neighbour: Issues in Interfaith Relations*, Geneva: World Council of Churches, p. 4.

3 See for example, Kenneth Cracknell, 2005, *In Good and Generous Faith: Christian Responses to Religious Pluralism*, Peterborough: Epworth Press.

4 Unpublished paper given at 'Being Christian and Living in a Multi Faith Society', St Albans Ecumenical Study Day, September 2007.

Glossary

The terms are Pāli unless otherwise indicated.

Akusala   unwholesome
Anattā   non-self, no unchanging essence within
Anicca   impermanence
Avijjā   ignorance
Bhāvanā   lit. bringing into being, meditation
Bhikkhu   Buddhist monk
Bhikkhuṇī   Buddhist nun
Bodhisatta (Skt Bodhisattva)   a Buddha-to-be
Brahmavihāras   lit. divine abiding, refers to four qualities: loving kindness, compassion, sympathetic joy and equanimity
Citta   usually translated as mind, but encompassing mind and heart; rational intellectual thought and the emotions connected with the heart
Dāna   an act of generosity, particularly generosity to the monastic Sangha
Dasa Sil Mātā   lit. ten precept mother; a contemporary Buddhist nun in Sri Lanka who follows a discipline of twelve rules.
Devale   a shrine to the gods found in Sri Lankan Buddhism
Dhamma (Skt Dharma)   the way things are, the Truth, the teaching of the Buddhas
Dharmakāya (Skt)   the dharma body of the Buddha (one of three 'bodies' of the Buddha developed in Mahāyāna Buddhism

Diṭṭhi   views, dogma, belief

Dosa   hatred

Dukkha   the pain and unsatisfactoriness of life

Hinayāna (Skt)   lit. lesser way, a derogatory name coined by Mahāyāna Buddhism for the Buddhism that predated it.

Jātaka   lit. birth stories, stories of the previous lives of the Buddha

Jhāna   meditative absorption, a heightened state of consciousness gained in *samatha* meditation

Kamma (Skt karma)   lit. action. The Law of Kamma states that wholesome action will have wholesome fruit and unwholesome action, unwholesome fruit.

Kāma   sensual enjoyment

Karuṇā   compassion

Kasina   an object for meditation, usually given by a meditation teacher

Kusala   wholesome

Lobha   greed

Mahāyāna (Skt)   lit. the Great Way; one of the two major divisions in world Buddhism

māna   pride, conceit, weighing oneself against another

mettā   loving kindness

moha   delusion

mud(itā   sympathetic joy, the ability to rejoice for a friend's success even if you have failed.

Nibbāna (Skt Nirvāṇa)   lit. extinction; the goal of the Buddhist path; the extinction of greed, hatred and delusion, deliverance from rebirth.

Nirodha   cessation

Pāramitā   lit. perfection, usually refers to ten perfections or moral qualities mastered by the Buddha-to-be

Paritta (Sinhala pirit)   lit. protection, usually refers to the chanting of a group of discourses (*suttas*) that are thought to bring protection

Paṭicca samuppāda   dependent arising, the arising of something because of something else

Pūja   veneration, devotional offering

Rāga   greed, lust, a synonym for *lobha*

Samādhi   concentration, one-pointedness of mind

Samatha   tranquillity, serenity (reached through concentration)

Saṃsāra   lit. continuous wandering, the process of birth, ageing, death and rebirth

Sangha   lit. community, usually refers, in Theravāda Buddhism, to communities of bhikkhus and bhikkhunīs

Sati   mindfulness

Satipaṭṭhāna   the foundations of mindfulness, traditionally a form of meditation that encourages mindfulness of body, feeling, and mind objects

Sīla   moral practice, code of morality

Sutta (Skt sutra)   lit. thread; a section of teaching, discourse, sermon

Taṇhā   craving, the chief root of suffering (*dukkha*)

Theravāda   lit. the Way of the Elders, one of the main divisions within world Buddhism.

Thūpa (Skt Stupa)   a monument erected over the remains/ relics of a holy being

Tipitaka   the threefold collection of canonical texts in Theravāda Buddhism

Upasampadā   lit. acquisition; higher ordination of a Buddhist monk or nun

Upekkhā   Equanimity

Vassa   lit. rain, usually refers to the rainy season when members of the monastic Sangha stay in one place

Vesakha   lit. the name of a month (April – May), refers to the Full Day when Buddhists commemorate the birth, enlightenment and death of the Buddha

Vihāra   lit. dwelling place, usually refers to the dwelling place of the monastic Sangha, similar to temple.

Vipassanā   insight, a form of meditation that fosters insight into reality

Virāga   lit. without lust, non-attachment

Viveka   physical withdrawal, seclusion

Further Reading

Buddhism

Bechert, H. and Gombrich, R., 1984, *The World of Buddhism*, London: Thames and Hudson.

Brazier, C., 2003, *Buddhist Psychology: Liberate your Mind, Embrace Life*, London: Robinson.

Gombrich, R., 2009, *What the Buddha Thought*, London: Equinox.

Gombrich, R., 1988, *Theravāda Buddhism: A Social History from Ancient Benares to Colombo*, London and New York: Routledge and Kegan Paul.

Harris, E. J., 1998, *What Buddhists Believe*, Oxford: Oneworld.

Harvey, P., 1990, *An Introduction to Buddhism: Teachings, History and Practices*, Cambridge: Cambridge University Press.

Kauth, R. and Harris, E. J., 2004, *Meeting Buddhists*, Leicester: Christians Aware.

Keown, D., 2000, *Buddhism: A Very Short Introduction*, Oxford: Oxford University Press.

McConnell, J. A., *Mindful Mediation: A Handbook for Buddhist Peacemakers*, Bangkok: Buddhist Research Institute, Mahachula University.

Nyanaponika Thera, 1968 (1980), *The Power of Mindfulness*, Kandy: Buddhist Publication Society.

Shaw, S., 2006, *Buddhist Meditation: An Anthology of Texts from the Pali Canon*, London and New York: Routledge.

Sivaraksa, S., 1994, *A Buddhist Vision for Renewing Society: Collected Articles by a Concerned Thai Intellectual*, Bangkok: The Inter-Religious Commission for Development.

171

Smart, N., 1989, *The World's Religions*, Cambridge and New York: Cambridge University Press.

Trainor, K., 2004, *Buddhism: The Illustrated Guide*, London: Duncan Baird.

Williams, P. with A. Tribe, 2000, *Buddhist Thought: A Complete Introduction to the Indian Tradition*, London and New York: Routledge.

Williams, P., 2008, *Mahāyāna Buddhism: The Doctrinal Foundations*, Abingdon: Routledge

Buddhist–Christian relations

Gross, R. M. and Muck, T. C., 2003, *Christians Talk about Buddhist Meditation; Buddhists Talk about Christian Prayer*, London and New York: Continuum.

Gross, R. and Radford Ruether, R., 2003, *Religious Feminism and the Future of the Planet: A Buddhist–Christian Conversation*, London and New York: Continuum.

Panikkar, R., 1989, *The Silence of God: The Answer of the Buddha*, Maryknoll, NY: Orbis.

Pieris, A., 1988, *Love Meets Wisdom: A Christian Experience of Buddhism*, Maryknoll, NY: Orbis.

Pieris, A., 1996, *Fire and Water: Basic Issues in Asian Buddhism and Christianity*, Maryknoll, NY: Orbis.

Nhat Hanh, T., 2007 (reprint) *Living Buddha, Living Christ*, Penguin Group (USA).

Schmidt-Leukel, P., 2005, *Buddhism and Christianity in Dialogue: The Gerald Weisfeld Lectures 2004*, London: SCM Press.

Schmidt-Leukel, P., G. Koberlin and J. Gotz, 2001, *Buddhist Perceptions of Jesus: Papers of the Third Conference of the European Network of Buddhist Christian Studies*, St Ottilien: EOS Verlag.

Inter faith relations

Ariarajah, S. W., 1999, *Not Without My Neighbour: Issues in Interfaith Relations*, Geneva: World Council of Churches.

Cracknell, K., 2005, *In Good and Generous Faith: Christian Responses to Religious Pluralism*, Peterborough: Epworth Press and Cleveland: Pilgrim Press.

Dupuis, J., 2003, *Christianity and the Religions: From Confrontation to Dialogue*, Maryknoll, NY: Orbis.

Eck, D., 2003, *Encountering God: A Spiritual Journey from Bozeman to Banares*, Boston: Beacon Press.

Faith Meeting Faith: Ways Forward in Inter-Faith Relations (A Resource for Individuals and Groups), 2004, Peterborough: Methodist Publishing House.

Torry, M. and Thorley, S. (eds), 2008, *Together and Different: Christians Engaging with People of Other Faiths*, Norwich: Canterbury Press.

Wingate, A., 2005, *Celebrating Difference, Staying Faithful: How to Live in a Multi-Faith World*, London: Darton, Longman & Todd.

Index

Lightning Source UK Ltd.
Milton Keynes UK
24 August 2010